THE LAME HORSE
Causes, Symptoms, and Treatment

THE LAME HORSE
Causes, Symptoms, and Treatment

James R. Rooney

Illustrated by Kathleen M. Friedenberg

Breakthrough PUBLICATIONS

MILLWOOD, NEW YORK 10546

Library of Congress Cataloging in Publication Data

Rooney, James R
 The lame horse: causes, symptoms, and treatment.

 1. Lameness in horses. I. Title.
SF959.L25R63 1973   636.1′08′9758   73-121
ISBN 0-914327-04-6

First Printing, January, 1974
Second Printing, March, 1975
Third Printing, January 1977
Fourth Printing, January, 1979
Fifth Printing, March, 1984
Sixth Printing, April, 1986

Notice To Readers

The procedures and recommendations contained in this book
should be undertaken only with the proper professional
supervision and accordingly publisher takes no responsibility
for the application of the contents of this book including
without limitation procedures, theories, and product
recommendations.

PRINTED IN THE UNITED STATES OF AMERICA

This book is dedicated to

STAN BERGSTEIN

who heeds voices crying in
the wilderness

CONTENTS

PREFACE

I shall attempt in this book to discuss many of the well-known types of lameness in the horse, considering the clinical signs, the cause of those clinical signs, the cause of the lesion, and what we might do to prevent and, in some instances, treat that lesion. Fact being fact, there are some lamenesses and some lesions about which we can do nothing, either to prevent or treat, given our present state of knowledge.

I shall assiduously avoid all mathematics. It will be necessary, however, to use a few vectors and a few very basic mechanical illustrations. It is, after all, impossible to talk about mechanics without talking about mechanics.

The horse, or any other living organism, may be considered a large-scale system with two primary goals: maintaining itself and reproducing itself. These two goals are subserved by the integrated functioning of many subsystems, each operating in a specific way to achieve a specific result. In order to completely understand the horse it would be necessary to understand the functioning of each of these subsystems both unto itself and in relation to all other subsystems. Needless to say, we are far from any such complete, integrated understanding.

In this book we shall be concerned with one subsystem of the horse, the locomotor system, lumping all the other subsystems into a category of "other." The cardiovascular, respiratory, and digestive systems are all essential to the locomotor function. I accept that and assume that they are operating properly and concentrate my attention on the locomotor mechanism.

The locomotor system may be defined as a mechanism—muscles, bones, joints, tendons, ligaments—subjected to an input, the force of gravity, and producing an output, movement (or the special case of movement: standing still) under the control of a regulating system: the central and peripheral nervous system.

9

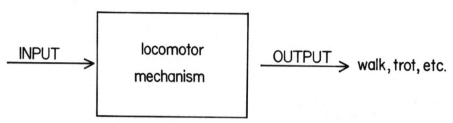

Fig. 1. Block diagram of the locomotor system.

The block diagram (Fig. 1) summarizes the system. In effect we have to consider three factors: input, locomotor mechanism, and output. The input, in turn, may be considered to have two components: (1) the signals going back and forth between the central nervous system and the locomotor system: sensory nerves telling the brain where the legs are and motor nerves causing the muscles to contract and change the position of the legs; (2) the input of gravity; that is, the load on the legs caused by the horse's body weight, the weight of the rider, sulky, or whatever. The output is, obviously, motion or standing still.

It will not be possible to cover everything in this book nor to delve into the many fine ramifications that have led to some of the ideas, hypotheses, and theories presented. For those who wish to go further I present, shamelessly, a list of my own books and where they can be obtained. Much of the material in those books is technical and rather heavy going for the general reader. Once you have mastered the present volume, however, you may well wish to go further, and I hope you will feel encouraged to do so.

Guide to the Dissection of the Horse. Dr. W. O. Sack, Department of Veterinary Anatomy, New York State Veterinary College, Ithaca, New York.

Biomechanics of Lameness in Horses. Williams and Wilkins Company, 428 East Preston Street, Baltimore, Maryland 21202.

Autopsy of the Horse. Williams and Wilkins Company, 428 East Preston Street, Baltimore, Maryland 21202.

Clinical Neurology of the Horse. KNA Press, Inc., Kennett Square, Pa. 19348.

ACKNOWLEDGMENTS

It is a pleasure for me to acknowledge my indebtedness to Nadine Browning for both typing the manuscript and for her thoughtful critiques. Dr. William Moyer read the entire manuscript and made many important suggestions. Neither of them are responsible for the contents, but they did their best!

Dr. Charles Reid kindly selected and provided the radiographs, teaching me a modicum of radiology in the process. Kathleen Friedenberg, the artist, has been more than patient. Her work speaks clearly for itself.

My thanks and apologies to those internes, residents and students who could not find me while this task was in progress.

I am indebted to the following journals, and their editors, for permission to reuse a number of illustrations that originally appeared in their publications: The Cornell Veterinarian, Veterinary Scope, Journal of the American Veterinary Medical Association, Williams and Wilkins Company, Baltimore, Maryland (Biomechanics of Lameness in Horses, 1969; Autopsy of the Horse, 1970), Hoof Beats, The Blood Horse.

Finally, I sincerely appreciate the good will and skillful work of the publisher, A. S. Barnes.

THE LAME HORSE
Causes, Symptoms, and Treatment

1
THE NORMAL FORELEG

BEFORE DISCUSSING THE VARIOUS LAMENESSES OF THE FORELEG, WE MUST take time to consider how the leg works normally. I shall use some technical terminology during the course of this discussion since many of the structures do not have common names. I shall indicate what these words mean and how they were derived. A number of pictures have been included, and you should refer to them frequently in order to gain an understanding of the relationships of the various anatomical structures and how they work.

First, examine Fig. 2. These are the bones of the foreleg and their names. Humans have all the same bones, with a few variations. The scapula is the shoulder blade, the humerus is the upper arm. In the human there are two bones in the forearm: the radius and the ulna. In the horse, the radius is still present, but the ulna has been reduced, partially lost. The upper end remains as the olecranon process (point of the elbow), and the lower end is fused with the radius to form part of the joint with the first row of carpal bones. The carpus is the same as the human wrist. In the horse it is often referred to as the knee, but it does not correspond to the human knee. Below the carpus the anatomy is considerably different from man. Man has five fingers, but the horse only has one main "finger" and two reduced ones. The thumb and the little finger have disappeared, the ring and index fingers are represented only by the narrow, slender splint bones, and the middle finger has become the longer and stronger third metacarpal bone or cannon bone (Fig. 3). At the knuckle, the fetlock joint of the horse, the cannon bone forms a joint with the upper end of the long pastern bone (phalanx 1). This bone joins with the short pastern bone (phalanx 2) which, in turn, articulates with the coffin

15

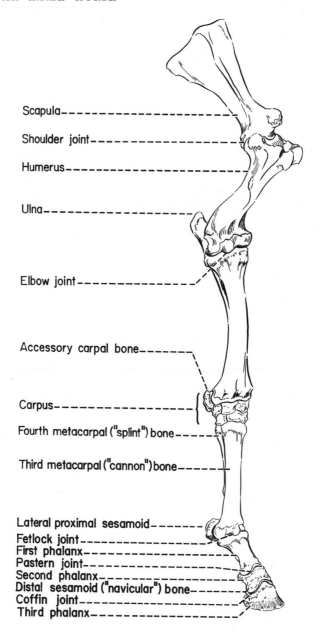

Scapula------------------------

Shoulder joint--------------------

Humerus------------------------

Ulna----------------------------

Elbow joint----------------------

Accessory carpal bone-----------

Carpus--------------------------

Fourth metacarpal ("splint") bone------

Third metacarpal ("cannon") bone------

Lateral proximal sesamoid---------
Fetlock joint---------------------
First phalanx---------------------
Pastern joint---------------------
Second phalanx--------------------
Distal sesamoid ("navicular") bone------
Coffin joint----------------------
Third phalanx---------------------

bone or pedal bone (phalanx 3). The fetlock joint is often called the "ankle," though, again, it does not correspond to the human ankle. A joint is called an articulation. The end of one bone articulates with the end of another bone. Each bone end is covered by smooth, lubricated, articular cartilage.

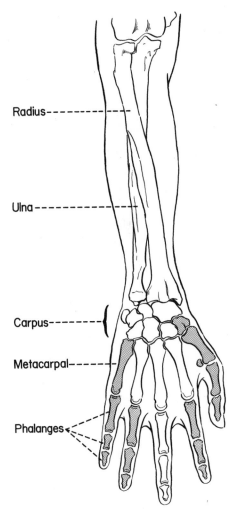

Radius- - - - - - - - -

Ulna- - - - - - - - - - -

Carpus- - - - - - - -

Metacarpal- - - - - -

Phalanges - - - - - -

Fig. 3. The bones of the human forearm, wrist, and hand. The horse has "lost" those bones which are shaded.

With this basic "bone" background we start with movement. The foot has just left the ground, and the horse must swing the leg forward in order to get it in position for the next stride, the next period of weight-bearing (Fig. 4). While a number of muscles cooperate to accomplish this protraction (pro = forward, traction = drag or pull), I shall show only a few to illustrate the point. The large, straplike brachiocephalicus pulls the leg forward (Fig. 4) (brachium = arm; cephalicus = head; thus, a muscle that runs from the arm to the head). At the same time the fan-shaped serratus muscle (serratus = serrated or toothlike, describing the appearance of the muscle, see Fig. 4)

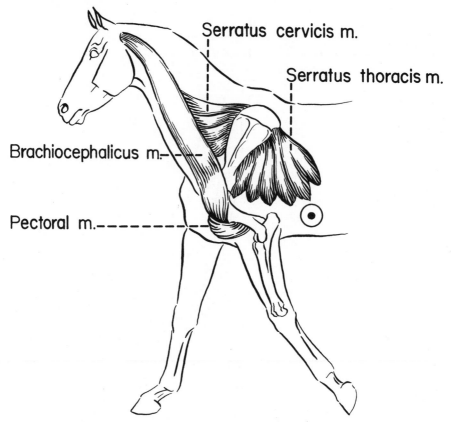

Fig. 4. Protraction (moving forward) of the foreleg of the horse. The brachiocephalicus pulls the leg forward. The contraction of the serratus thoracis assists by rotating the leg forward around a point near the center of the humerus. The serratus cervicis and latissimus dorsi are relaxing. The center of gravity is shown as the "bullseye."

undergoes some rather complicated maneuvering. This big muscle is the main support or attachment of the foreleg to the body. As you can see in Fig. 5 the serratus forms a sling in which the chest hangs between the two forelegs. Returning to Fig. 4, the serratus is composed of two parts: the serratus cervicis (cervicis = cervical or neck part) and the serratus thoracis (thoracis = thoracic or chest part).

As the brachiocephalicus is pulling the leg forward, the serratus thoracis is also contracting, pulling down and back on the upper end of the scapula. Since the center of rotation for this forward movement of the leg is near the middle of the humerus the down and back pull on the scapula helps to rotate the leg forward. The center of rotation is near the middle of the humerus because the pectoral (pectoral =

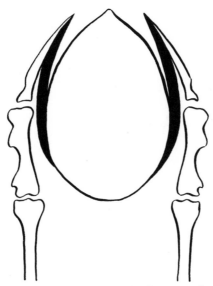

Fig. 5. A head-on view of the chest with the scapula, humerus, and part of radius shown on both sides. The heavy, black bands represent the serratus muscle, suspending the chest in a sling between the two forelegs.

breast or chest) muscles run from the chest to hook on to the humerus near the middle.

While the serratus thoracis is contracting, the serratus cervicis is relaxing. This is quite obvious if one studies the illustrations. The scapula could not move unless one part of the muscle relaxes while the other part is contracting. This is known as *reciprocal muscle action* and is an important aspect of all muscle activity anywhere in the body. Simply put, whenever one muscle contracts there is another muscle that must relax (Fig. 6). Reciprocal action of muscles provides not only the ability to move the bone in opposite directions, but also smooths or dampens the movement of the bone, preventing jerky, irregular action. This is a very important function of muscles, and is directly related to many forms of lameness. If you will construct the simple model shown in Fig. 7, you can demonstrate the action for yourself. Hang a string with a weight on the end. Jerk on the other string tied to the weight. The weight will move and swing about. Now tie an elastic cord to the weight and to something else, the wall, a chair. Jerk the weight again. Its pendulum swinging will be much smoother; it will not vibrate. The elastic cord represents the muscle and its ability to dampen vibration.

As the leg swings forward it flexes or bends at the carpus. This is

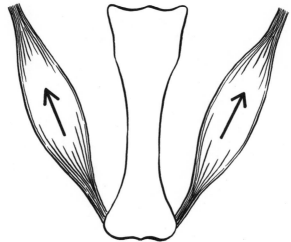

Fig. 6. *A simplified illustration of the reciprocal action of two muscles on a bone. When one muscle contracts, the other relaxes and vice versa.*

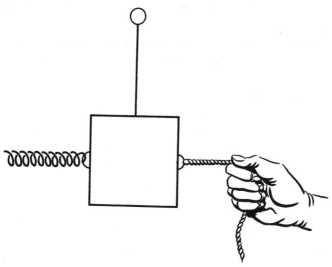

Fig. 7. *Model to demonstrate the damping, smoothing action of muscles. If the rope is replaced by an elastic band the swinging about of the weight will be reduced, damped.*

a very useful labor-saving device for the horse or the human. Try running without flexing your knee; you will quickly fatigue. The muscle force which the horse must use to swing the leg forward is, in part, a function of the length of the leg: the longer the leg, the more force required. Shortening the leg by flexing it, then, reduces the effective length and, thereby, the force necessary to move it forward. In mechanical terms this is called reduction of the moment of inertia of the leg.

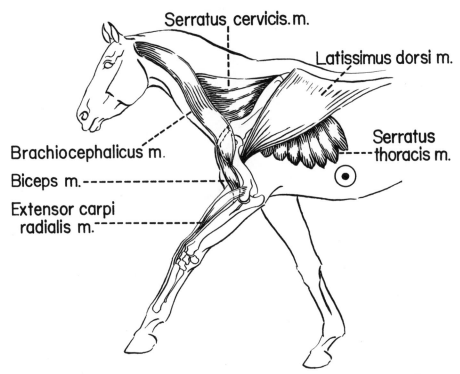

Fig. 8. Protraction of foreleg nearly completed. Carpus is extending.

Now the leg is almost fully protracted (Fig. 8). The muscles of the forearm, particularly the extensor carpi radialis, assist the simple swinging movement of the leg by extending the carpus in preparation for putting the foot on the ground (extensor carpi radialis = the muscle that extends or straightens the carpus on the radius). We shall call this "putting of the foot on the ground," an awkward phrase at best, *impact*. Once the leg is fully protracted, the serratus cervicis begins to contract while the serratus thoracis relaxes. The brachiocephalicus also relaxes while its reciprocal muscle, the latissimus dorsi, contracts (latissimus dorsi = the widest muscle of the back, a description of the shape of the muscle).

The leg swings down and back, retracting (pulling back). The foot impacts with the ground while the leg is moving backward. This is extremely important. If the leg is swinging back at the same speed the horse's body is moving forward, the horse is running at near constant speed, and the only load applied to the leg by the horse's body weight is straight down. If he wants to run slower, he slows

Fig. 9. A horse, somewhat surprised, suspended at his center of gravity.

down the speed of the backward swing of the leg. Obviously, if he wants to run faster, he retracts the leg faster. With the exception of the sudden sliding stops of the cow pony, the foot is always retracting when it impacts.

The body weight of the horse is now applied to the foreleg, and the leg must sustain or support that weight as well as try to move it forward. For mechanical purposes, the weight of the horse is considered to be concentrated at a single point, the center of gravity. In simplest terms, the center of gravity is that point where the horse could be suspended and balanced (Fig. 9). The center of gravity of a stick or ruler is that point where the stick is balanced when supported at only that point (Fig. 10). It is clear that the pull exerted by the weight of the horse, acting at the center of gravity, will tend to pull the leg down and back, a tendency that must be resisted. As can be seen in Fig. 4, the pull of the center of gravity acting through the serratus thoracis will move the scapula down and back, flexing or closing the angle of the shoulder joint. This movement is resisted by the biceps brachii (biceps = two heads; brachii = arm: a description of the appearance of the muscle) as well as by the contraction of the serratus cervicis. The elbow joint will also tend to flex, in the opposite direction but for the same reason, and this is resisted by the powerful mass of the triceps brachii (tri-ceps = three-headed muscle).

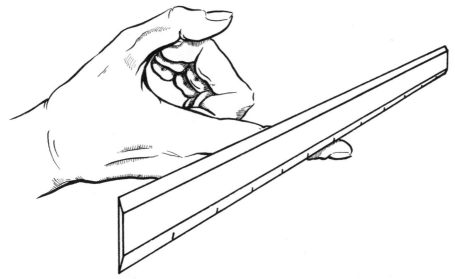

Fig. 10. A rule is balanced on the finger when supported at its center of gravity.

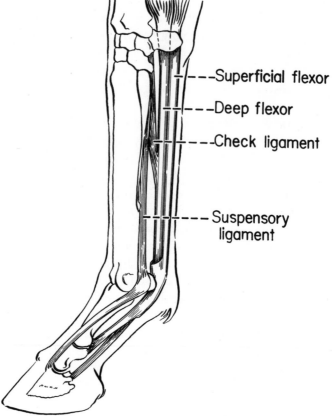

Fig. 11. *Suspensory ligament and flexor tendons which resist rotation of coffin and fetlock joints.*

The body weight forces the fetlock and coffin joints to flex, and that flexion (rotation) is resisted by the powerful suspensory ligament and the flexor tendons (Fig. 11). The horse is unique in having so-called check ligaments attached to both the superficial and deep flexor tendons. This means that the rotation of the coffin and fetlock can be resisted without any muscle action whatsoever. In fact, the major function of all the muscles of the forearm is not to cause movement but, rather, to prevent it. (The flexor muscles assist the tendon-check ligament system to prevent movement; their primary job is to prevent rather than cause movement.)

All of these actions are obviously designed to receive and support the body weight: shock absorption. Following immediately upon that extremely important function, however, the foreleg must also con-

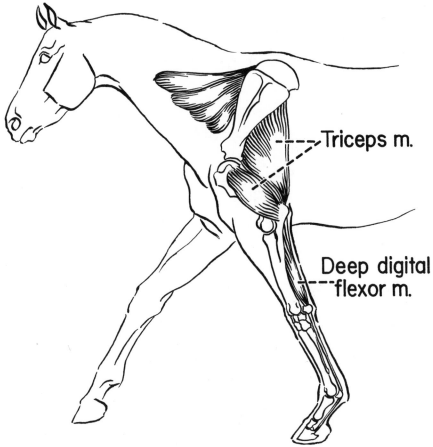

Triceps m.

Deep digital flexor m.

Fig. 12. Propulsion by the foreleg. The serratus cervicis (in front of scapula, not labeled), triceps, and deep digital flexor are major propulsion muscles, moving the leg back.

tribute to the forward movement, or propulsion, of the horse. It is true that the primary functions of the forelegs are to support weight, absorb shock, and lift the animal from the ground for the flight phase of the stride, while the rearleg provides the main propulsion. The secondary function of the foreleg is to assist in moving the horse forward. Referring to Fig. 12, the serratus cervicis and the powerful triceps seem to be the major agents in pushing the leg to the rear and, consequently, the body forward. Toward the end of the stride, just before the hoof clears the ground, the large deep flexor muscle provides a strong pull on the hoof, lifting the horse up and forward.

This has been an all too brief, thumbnail sketch of the very complicated action of the foreleg. Further details of the action of the several parts of the leg will be brought out as I discuss the lamenesses that affect those parts. For now you may wish to stop reading and build a model that will illustrate the points that have been discussed (Fig. 13).

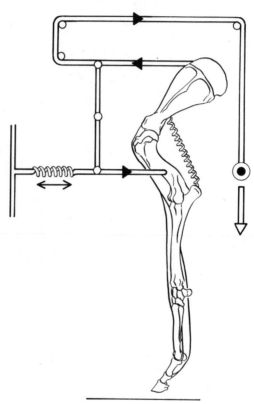

Fig. 13. Model of foreleg. Elastic bands, springs, and a "center of gravity" are provided. As the center of gravity is pulling down, the leg retracts. When the center of gravity is moved up, the spring at left (the brachiocephalicus) will protract the leg.

2
FORELEG LAMENESS

A FEW INTRODUCTORY REMARKS ARE IN ORDER. *Lameness* IS A CLINICAL sign or set of signs by which the horse tells us that he feels pain or discomfort in a given leg. A *lesion* is the specific damage to a part of the leg which causes such pain or discomfort. We usually recognize *acute lesions* and *chronic lesions.* The former are of short duration and characterized by pain, heat, swelling, and (when recognizable) reddening of the affected part. Chronic lesions are frequently rather difficult to recognize. The same signs are often present, but they may be considerably less obvious.

What I shall do in the succeeding pages is to discuss the specific lesions that cause lameness, what we know of their cause, and how they may be diagnosed, prevented, and treated. Needless to say the stories will often be incomplete; we do not have all the answers. We shall start at the top of the leg and work our way down.

SWEENY

The shoulder joint is the only one in the horse's body that does not have ligaments to hold it in proper position. Instead, the joint is surrounded by muscles that both guide the movement of the joint as well as hold it together. The three main muscles are the subscapularis, the supraspinatus, and the infraspinatus. Subscapularis means beneath the scapula, in this case, between the scapula and the chest wall. This muscle is not involved in sweeny and will not be considered further. Spinatus refers to the spine of the scapula while supra means above and infra below. Therefore, supraspinatus means the muscle above the spine of the scapula and infraspinatus the muscle below the spine of the scapula (Fig. 14). Both of these muscles are innervated by a motor nerve called the suprascapular nerve (Fig. 14). If the suprascapular nerve is damaged, these two muscles cannot contract, just as a light bulb will not light if the wire is torn in half. Muscles that have been deprived of their motor nerve will (unlike a light bulb) atrophy (wither up and shrink).

When the nerve is first damaged, the clinical signs may be difficult to pin down. If the animal is watched from in front, moving toward

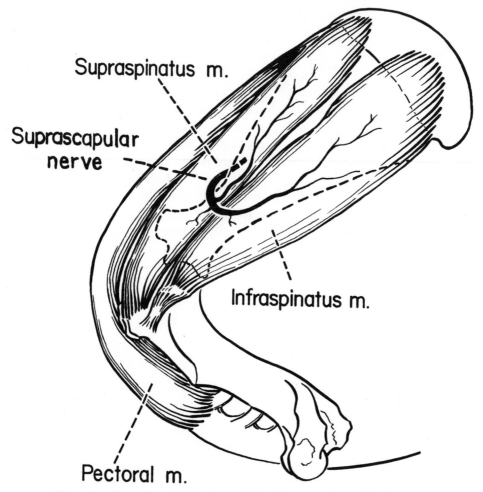

Fig. 14. Scapula and humerus. The first muscle to the left is a pectoral muscle, then the supraspinatus, and, finally, the infraspinatus. The suprascapular nerve and its branches to the two muscles are shown.

the observer, the shoulder may snap or pop outward as weight is put on the leg. The forward phase (protraction) of the stride is shortened. This is logical since the two muscles that are there to prevent such outward movement of the shoulder joint are not functioning. In a short time the diagnosis becomes very obvious with the onset of marked atrophy of the two muscles, i.e., the muscle mass shrinks.

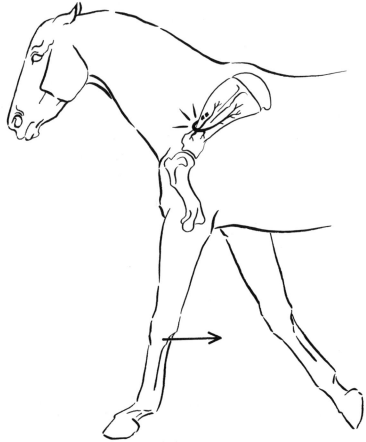

Fig. 15. Sudden slipping backward of the foreleg will tense, overstretch, and damage the suprascapular nerve.

The cause of the suprascapular nerve damage is sudden slipping back of the shoulder from the protracted position (Fig. 15). This slipping causes tension in the nerve, and the tension, in turn, either tears the nerve fibers or damages their blood supply, so that the nerve undergoes necrosis (dies). This type of slipping of the leg usually occurs on slippery or wet ground when the horse is pulling a heavy load, clambering up a steep grade, etc. Sweeny was particularly common in the days of draft horses working on wet, hard streets or in wet, muddy ground during the early spring plowing.

There is no effective or even rational treatment for sweeny. Only time will tell if the damage has been so severe that the nerve will not regenerate. To be perfectly honest, it usually does not. The sweenied horse is obviously at a disadvantage compared to the normal animal but often still can be used for moderate work and, of course, is completely suitable for breeding, other factors being equal. Prevention is obvious: do not work horses on wet, slippery ground. If you feel that you must work on bad going, either remove the shoes or use a very thin, light shoe which will allow the hoof to cut into the ground, preventing slipping. This is a point which I shall refer to time and again. The horse's hoof is designed to cut into the ground and anything that prevents it, such as hard going and/or the web of the horseshoe, is distinctly not good for the horse.

You may well be advised, as you desperately shop around for some treatment, to have the horse's shoulder injected with an internal blister. I doubt very much that internal blisters do much good for anything, but I can guarantee that they do not assist in nerve regeneration. The blister may increase the scar tissue content of the area, providing a cosmetic but not a functional result.

BICIPITAL BURSITIS

The biceps brachii is a powerful and important muscle that helps to control the movement of both the shoulder and elbow joints and, somewhat indirectly, the carpus. Where the muscle curves around in front of the shoulder joint (Fig. 16) it is enclosed in a fluid-filled sac called the bicipital bursa (bicipital is the adjective for biceps). We shall encounter a number of bursae as we go along and should say a word about them now. They are sacs that surround the tendons of muscles and contain synovial, lubricating fluid. They are generally found wherever the normal movement of a tendon is around a turn and help to provide lubrication, easing that turning or curving movement.

Acute inflammation of the bicipital bursa is characterized by severe supporting and swinging leg lameness. That is, the animal shows pain when bearing weight on the leg (to the point, perhaps, of being "three-legged lame") and, also, when the leg is not bearing

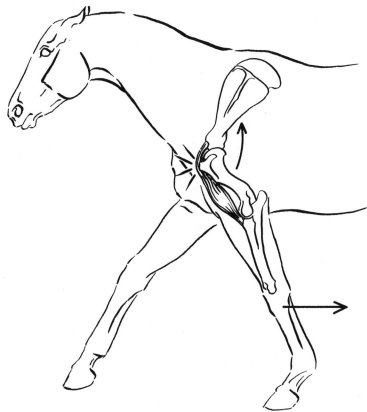

Fig. 16. Slipping backward of the foreleg while the shoulder joint is flexing (arrow) and the elbow is extending tenses and damages the tendon of the biceps. The biceps is the only muscle shown.

weight, swinging through the air. The animal may refuse to move the leg forward past the other leg but will move it back. He may attempt to fix the shoulder and elbow joints in order to prevent any movement whatsoever. As a result, there is marked lifting of the head and imperfect flexion of the shoulder and elbow joints when the horse is moving forward. This may appear as stumbling. The clinical signs may be somewhat less obvious in the more chronic case, but pain can be elicited by pulling the leg upward and backward. One can occasionally elicit a painful reaction by deep manipulation of the biceps area.

The cause of bicipital bursitis is indicated in Fig. 16. The leg slips backward while the shoulder joint is flexing and the elbow joint extending. With sweeny, the leg slips back from the protracted position, while with bicipital bursitis, the leg slips back from the retracted position. This slipping causes great tension in the biceps tendon within the bursa, and this tension tears tissue, resulting in acute inflammation.

As you might expect, this condition was more common in draft horse days, for the same reasons already detailed for sweeny. Direct trauma, a blow, to the front of the shoulder is often suggested as the cause of this condition (and sweeny). This is nonsense since there is a heavy coating of pectoral muscle over the front of the shoulder, and we should expect severe damage to this muscle before seeing damage to either the bursa or the nerve—and we do not see such muscle damage.

The diagnosis can be firmly established by injecting an anesthetic solution or steroid-anesthetic combination into the bicipital bursa. The steroid has the advantage of relieving the inflammation and thus the pain. It must be strongly emphasized, as I shall do repeatedly, that steroids should not be injected repeatedly; and that adequate rest must be allowed following such injection before the animal is returned to work. The advice of a veterinarian is essential, and the prognosis for return to full work following adequate rest is, in general, quite good. Several cases have responded very nicely to a regimen of oral phenylbutazolidin. Preventive measures are the same as those given for sweeny.

FRACTURE OF THE SCAPULA

Fracture of this well-protected bone is not common but should be mentioned for the sake of completeness. One of the most common types is shown in Fig. 17. The fractures may occur as the result of a misstep by the horse or as a result of a direct blow, such as falling heavily to one side. Surgical repair has not been too successful, and only "wait and see" can be used for treatment. The horse is usually dead lame on the leg. Only large, veterinary X-ray machines can show these fractures. With the fracture shown in Fig. 17 the horse may eventually become sound. The other fracture, through the main part of the scapula, is, for all practical purposes, hopeless.

SHOULDER LAMENESS

This is an extraordinarily vague entity, if it exists at all. As a very wise, careful observer, J. A. W. Dollar, said, "The diagnosis of shoulder lameness chiefly depends on the negative results of local examination; the more careful the local examination, the rarer will be the

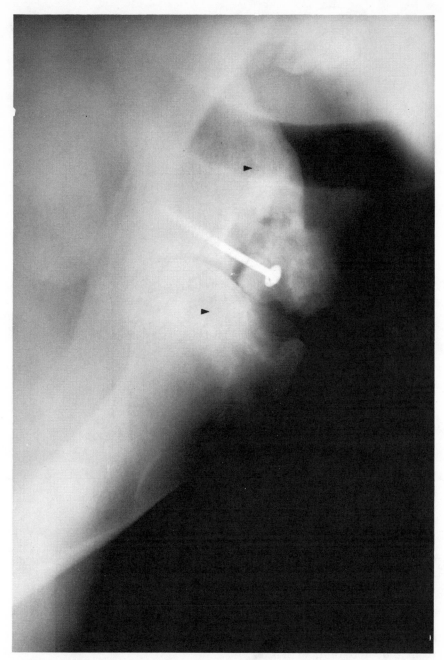

Fig. 17. Radiograph of one type of scapular fracture which has been repaired with a screw. Upper arrow is on the scapula and lower is on the upper end of humerus.

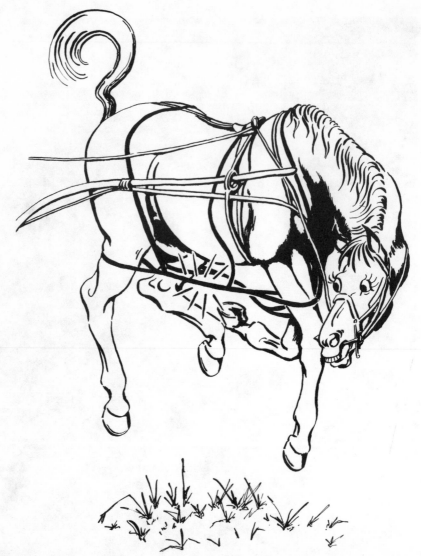

Fig. 18. Harness horse, new to the hobbles, moving foreleg forward and rearleg backward simultaneously (trying to trot). Such a movement may strain the muscles of the shoulder.

diagnosis shoulder lameness." Most shoulder-muscle sore horses suffer from foot and/or heel lamenesses.

The clinical signs associated with this condition are those already given for bicipital bursitis: reluctance or refusal to move the shoulder joint. In my autopsy experience, sweeny, bicipital bursitis, scapular fractures, and severe acute or chronic infection of the joint in foals have been the only significant causes of lameness associated with the shoulder.

Harness horses may show transient pain in the shoulder area as a result of the hobbles used to keep pacers on gait. The obvious example is the trotter who is being converted to the pace. While he is learning to move both legs on the same side, instead of his natural diagonal gait, mistakes can be made: the front leg trying to protract while the rearleg on the same side is retracting (Fig. 18). Such a miscalculation can put severe strain on the muscles of the shoulder area, resulting in pain of variable degrees of severity. Similarly, hobbles that are too tight may force the animal to stay on stride, and thus restrict the movements of either the fore or rearleg, resulting in vague signs of muscle strain.

RADIAL NERVE PARALYSIS

This is an occasional cause of severe lameness in horses. The radial nerve innervates those muscles which cause extension of the elbow (the triceps brachii) and extension of the carpus and digit (the extensor carpi radialis, for one) (Fig. 19). The clinical signs may be summarized:

1. The foot is moved forward (protracted) normally but because of the loss of function of the triceps, the horse cannot extend the elbow joint and straighten the leg to the normal position for supporting weight.

2. If the animal moves slowly on a smooth surface, nothing may be noted. If an obstacle is encountered, however, the foot is not able to lift sufficiently and will strike the obstacle.

3. With complete paralysis, the animal stands with the shoulder and elbow dropped and the carpus and digit flexed. The toe may be the only portion of the foot resting on the ground. (Fig. 20).

4. The triceps muscle, and other muscles innervated by the radial nerve, may eventually atrophy.

The cause of radial paralysis is damage to the radial nerve of the same type that was discussed with sweeny. The radial nerve is overstretched and necrosis occurs. In this case, however, the radial nerve is damaged when the foot slips forward. The radial nerve wraps around the humerus from inside to outside and is put under severe tension when the shoulder joint is overextended, as when the leg slips forward. The other two major nerves of the foreleg, the median and ulnar, do not wrap around the humerus and can slide forward without being subjected to excessive tension.

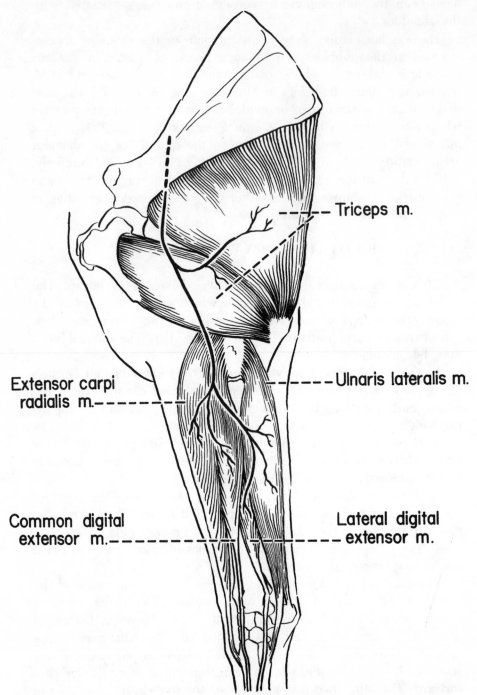

Triceps m.

Extensor carpi
radialis m.

Ulnaris lateralis m.

Common digital
extensor m.

Lateral digital
extensor m.

Fig. 19. The radial nerve ramifying to the extensor muscles of the foreleg.

Fig. 20. Complete radial paralysis.

Radial paralysis was quite common in draft horses and in carriage horses working on wet, cobbled streets. Today it is most frequent in young horses, particularly rambunctious yearling colts, racing and playing in wet and/or snowy fields. I am sure you have all seen the acrobatic sliding stops such animals can make when running full blast up to a fence (Fig. 21). It is this type of movement that can overextend the leg and damage the radial nerve.

Radial paralysis is said to occur following casting animals for surgical procedures. Actually this is a mixed nerve paralysis, the signs of radial paralysis overshadowing those of median and ulnar paralysis. Such damage is due to impaired blood supply to the nerves as a result of the animal lying on one side for a prolonged period. Such a disorder is transient as a rule.

Fig. 21. The type of sliding stop that can overstretch the radial nerve and lead to radial paralysis.

Fractures of the humerus may also cause radial nerve damage. Usually, nerve damage of this type is irreversible. Obviously, nerve damage in combination with a fracture is a total disaster.

Radial paralysis cannot be treated except by tincture of time. Many cases will return to normal within a few months, but a few will be permanently disabled.

FRACTURE OF THE HUMERUS

Fractures of the humerus are one of the more common long bone fractures of the horse. They are, in my experiences, always spiral fractures (Figs. 22, 23), occurring as a result of severe twisting of the bone. Most humeral fractures occur because the animal places the leg improperly while running, even at moderate rates of speed. The foot is either placed too far under the animal or, more frequently, too far out to the side. In either case severe twisting forces are applied to the bone and fracture may result. While some horses fracture

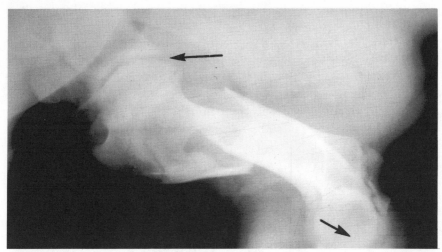

Fig. 22. *Radiograph of fracture of the humerus. The upper left arrow indicates the shoulder joint and the lower right arrow the elbow joint.*

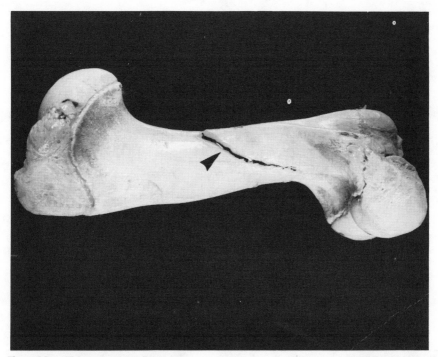

Fig. 23. *Fracture of the humerus. The arrow head points to the black line, indicating the spiral fracture.*

simply running about in the field, many occur while the horse is being ridden. The rider forces the animal to make a very sudden, sharp turn, and he places the leg too far out to one side in an attempt to maintain his balance (Fig. 24). A horse can be taught to make such sharp turns, but he must be taught and not simply jerked to one side whenever the rider wishes.

Surgical repair is the only real hope for such animals, and it is, with our present state of skill and knowledge, not too often successful.

Fig. 24. The rider has suddenly jerked the horse to his left. The horse reaches out with the left foreleg in order to catch himself. Such a misstep is a frequent cause of fracture of the humerus.

ELBOW JOINT

This joint is singularly immune to significant clinical damage. If a horse is lame in one front leg, he quite regularly develops scoring or wear lines in the opposite elbow joint (Fig. 25). Such minor damage to the joint is, so far as we know, completely silent clinically.

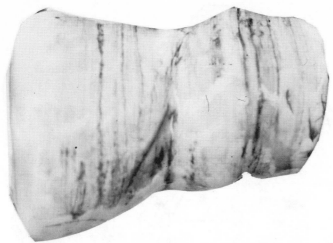

Fig. 25. Scoring lines on the humeral part of the elbow joint. The lines have been emphasized by pouring dye on the joint surface.

FRACTURE OF THE OLECRANON PROCESS

The olecranon process has already been described as the persistent upper end of the ulna. The powerful triceps muscle attaches to this process. Fracture of the process occasionally occurs in either foals or older horses. In foals the fracture usually is through the epiphyseal plate. In older horses the fracture is through the neck of the olecranon process (Fig. 26). This fracture probably occurs because the animal gets into the position shown in Fig. 27, the leg too far forward, the body dropping, and the triceps contracting strongly, trying to pull the leg back.

Such fractures are very difficult to handle. External splints are ineffective, and surgical procedures, the insertion of bone plates and/ or screws, must be resorted to. Even with the best of surgical skill, however, the prognosis is poor because triceps contraction tends to pull the fracture apart.

SHOE BOIL

This is a swelling of variable size that appears over the point of the elbow. Normally, there is a small bursa between the skin and the olecranon process. This bursa facilitates movement of the skin over the bone just as other bursae, such as the bicipital, facilitate movement of tendons over bone. If this bursa is irritated and becomes

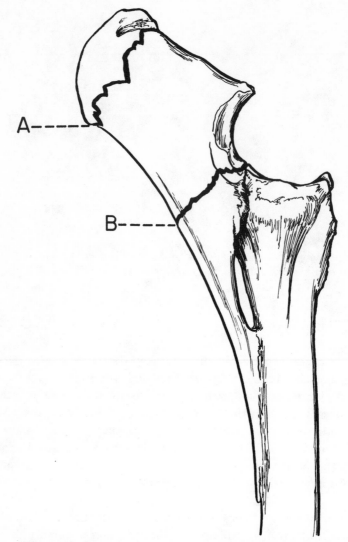

A------

B------

Fig. 26.   The upper end of the radius and the olecranon process. Foals generally fracture at A, while older horses fracture at B.

inflamed, the amount of fluid in the bursa increases, and the large swelling that results is called a shoe boil.

The shoe boil is caused either by chronic irritation from a horse lying with his heel and shoe pressed against the bursa or because of high action (Hackney ponies, for example), the leg folding so markedly that the heel or the shoe strikes the point of the elbow.

Prevention obviously entails trimming the horse's foot properly,

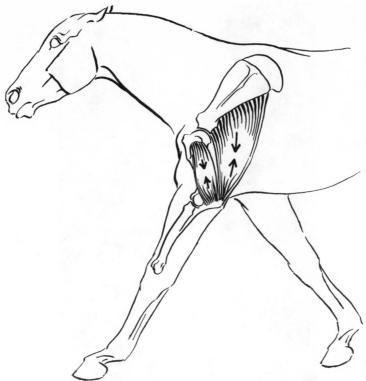

Fig. 27. The mechanism of olecranon process fracture. The leg is forward and the triceps is contracting strongly to pull it back.

avoiding long trailers on the shoe, not demanding or encouraging the horse to fold his leg to such an extreme, and elbow boots (awkward, sloppy things at best). Shoe boil is obviously a man-made disorder (we shall see quite a few more!). If shoeing is properly done, and the hyperaction of the show pony is avoided, the problem could virtually disappear.

Treatment is not very satisfactory. The cause or causes should be removed. Careful draining of fluid and steroid injection by a veterinarian may help, but this is usually of no value unless done early before the swelling becomes very large.

FRACTURE OF THE RADIUS

The radius is quite free of any significant problems other than fracture. While the bone can break in several different ways, the most common is bending or twisting failure near the middle (Fig. 28).

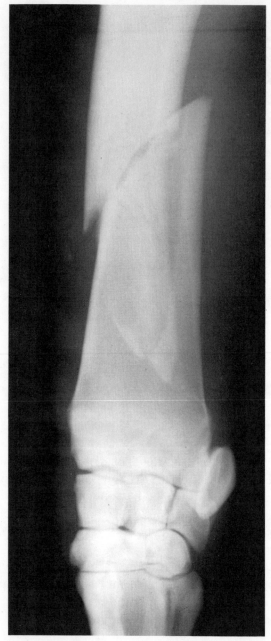

Fig. 28.   Fracture of the radius near the middle. The carpus is at the bottom of the picture.

External splints can be used, particularly in foals, but surgical repair with bone plates and screws may be necessary in most cases.

EPIPHYSITIS

This is a common condition in young horses. It has been given a variety of names, including rickets. All the names are misnomers, but rickets is surely the worst since there has never been a bona fide case of rickets described in horses. Epiphysitis literally means an inflammation of the epiphysis, the end of a long bone. Actually the lesion is in the epiphyseal plate and is not an inflammation at all. Before I go any further, I should define epiphyseal plate. Long bones grow in two different ways: by an increase in diameter and by an increase in length. The increase in length is accomplished by growth of the epiphyseal plate, which is then converted to bone. Each epiphyseal plate has its own particular life span. For example, the one at the lower end of the cannon bone stops growing and disappears around seven to twelve months of age in light breeds of horses (somewhat later on average in cold bloods), while the one at the lower end of the radius closes as the animal nears two years of age.

So called epiphysitis is characterized by the development of slight lameness and a pronounced swelling at the lower end of the inside of the cannon bone and the upper end of the long pastern bone in the animal that is approaching one year of age. It also occurs at the lower end of the inside of the radius, just above the carpus, in the animal nearing two years of age. It rarely occurs in the rearleg and, then, only at the lower end of the cannon bone.

The lameness, as a rule, disappears rather quickly while the enlargement may persist as a blemish for some time.

The lesion is a crushing and destruction of part of the epiphyseal cartilage plate with the subsequent formation of new bone in an attempt to stabilize the destroyed area. In essence this is an epiphyseal fracture and, as with all bone fractures, the body responds by laying down new bone in an attempt to repair the fracture. This new bone is the enlargement that one sees in the live horse (Figs. 29–33).

For reasons too complicated to go into here it is quite clear that the cause of the crushing or fracture of the cartilage is excessive weight. This may come about because the bone is deformed, a markedly toed-in conformation causing too great a load on the inside of the leg, for example. Most commonly, however, it is simply a matter of overfeeding the young, growing horse. The skeletal system grows at a fixed, predetermined rate set up by the hereditary makeup of that particular horse. We cannot, by any reasonable means, speed up or slow down the rate at which bones grow. We can, on the other hand, put plenty of fat on the young horse by feeding him heavily

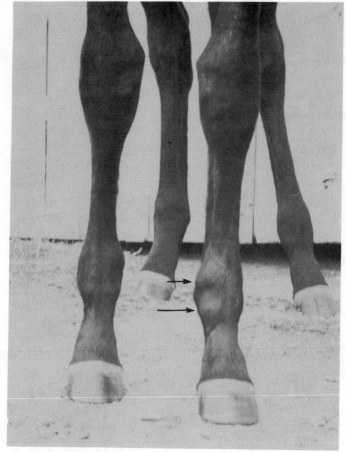

Fig. 29. Bony enlargement at lower end of cannon (upper arrow) and upper end of the long pastern bone (lower arrow). So-called epiphysitis.

in order to make him look slick and fat for showing or sales purposes. We put so much lard on the young horse that he is, for all practical purposes, too fat for the size of his bones. In particular, we can put on more weight than the epiphyseal plates are built to resist; hence, they crush. A similar condition occurs in swine and cattle being heavily fed for market. The question is, then, do you want a sound horse to ride and work or do you want to fatten him up and eat him!

A clear example of this problem is the Quarter Horse with his large, heavy body and light legs. Epiphysitis is quite common in this type of unbalanced horse.

A great deal of rubbish has been purveyed about the cause of this epiphyseal damage. Everything from protein to vitamin D to estrogen

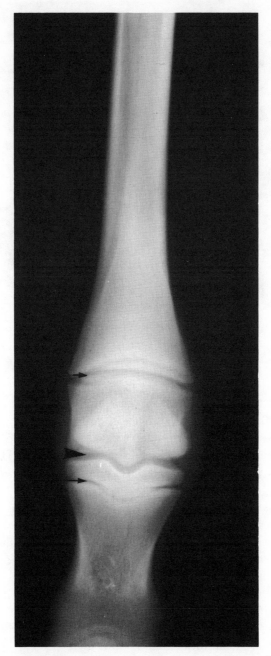

Fig. 30.   Radiograph of fetlock region of a normal young horse, showing an epiphyseal plate at the lower end of the cannon bone (upper arrow), the fetlock joint (middle arrow), and the epiphyseal plate at the upper end of the long pastern bone (lower arrow).

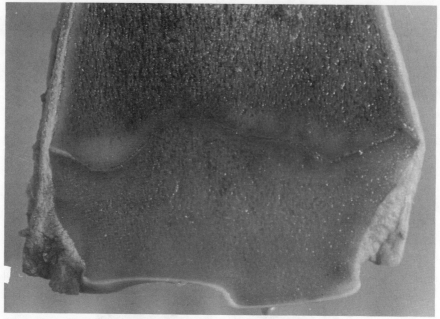

Fig. 31. The lower end of the radius of a young horse showing the normal, wavy epiphyseal plate.

have been blamed at one time or another, with no facts to support the contentions. If one will, however, properly trim feet and raise young horses like horses rather than beef cattle, the incidence of epiphysitis can be markedly decreased. The Quarter Horse problem is a serious one. Only breed standards emphasizing a proper relationship between body size and leg size can help them.

Epiphysitis is not a serious lesion, as a rule, because the damage usually occurs close to the time the epiphyseal plate is closing, ceasing to grow. As a result, the enlargement tends to decrease with time and eventually disappear with no untoward after-effects.

Occasionally, a young animal develops a severe, three-legged lameness, such as radial paralysis or fracture of a foreleg. Routinely, epiphysitis will develop in the other foreleg because of the increased weight-bearing by the other foreleg. Also, a foal may be born with a congenital malformation of one or both legs so severe that excessive pressure is put on the inside of the leg; needless to say epiphysitis appears in such animals as well.

How do you treat an animal with this condition? I hope the answer is obvious: put him on a diet!

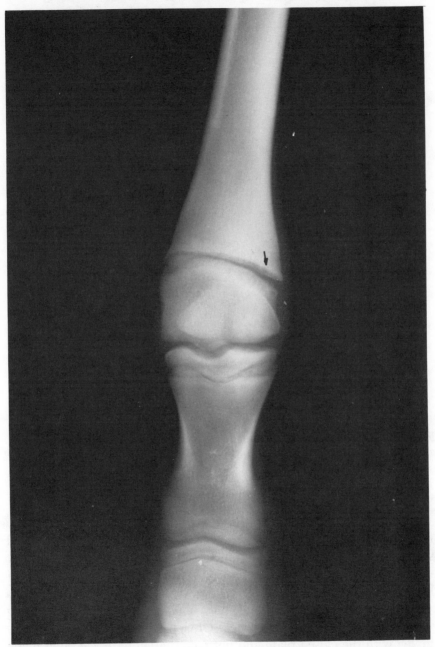

Fig. 32.   Radiograph showing widening and irregularity of the cannon bone epiphyseal plate (arrow) on the inside of the leg.

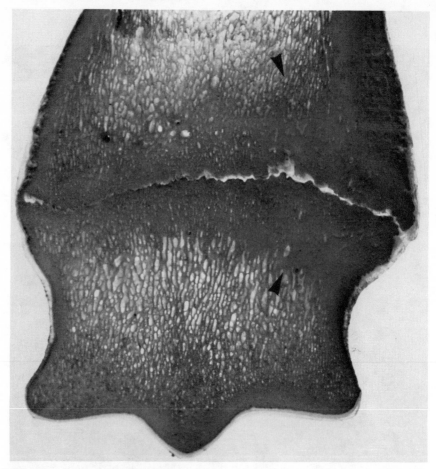

Fig. 33. A transilluminated postmortem specimen of epiphyseal plate damage. The new bone is indicated by arrows. The epiphyseal plate is widened (white) and broken up on the right, the inside of the leg.

X-raying the lower end of the radius has achieved some notoriety if not popularity as a means of determining whether a two year old is ready to train and race. In essence, the X-ray indicates whether or not the epiphyseal plate has closed and is, therefore, a means of determining the age of the horse. Certainly some horses close this plate earlier than others. In fact, they may close the plate in one leg before they do in the opposite leg. Obviously, then, one should race the leg with the closed plate and not race the leg with the open plate. Let me know how you make out. The best determinant of when a horse should be trained and raced is not an X-ray; it is the careful, considered, intelligent evaluation of the trainer.

CARPUS

Damage to the carpus or "knee" has become one of the most important causes of lameness in the modern racehorse, whatever the breed. The knee joint is actually composed of three joints in close proximity (Fig. 34). The lower end of the radius articulates with the proximal (upper) row of carpal bones. The upper row, in turn, articulates with the lower row of carpal bones, and the lower row articulates with the upper end of the cannon bone.

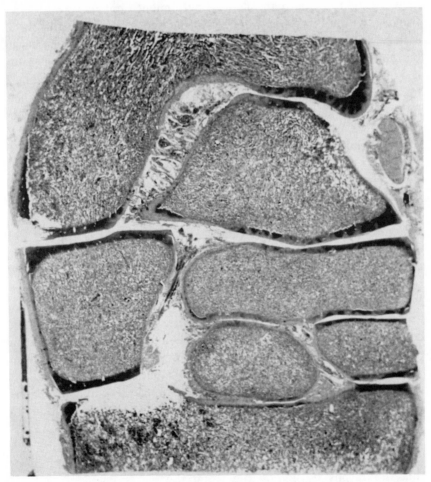

Fig. 34. Low power picture of a section of a horse's knee. The upper piece of bone is the lower end of the radius, and the lower piece is the upper end of the cannon bone. The smaller bones in between are the several rows of carpal bones.

Each row of carpal bones contains four separate bones, but we shall only be concerned with three in each row, the ones responsible for most of the significant functions of this compound joint. Each of these small bones is actually a box of interwoven fine trabeculae or strands of bone enclosed in a thin bony shell (Fig. 34). They are not solid blocks of concrete. Each time the foreleg strikes the ground, large forces are applied to the carpal bones, and one might guess these bones would be very hard and sturdy to resist these large forces. On the contrary, the spongy, woven nature of the bones makes them quite resilient and elastic. They may be likened to the box springs on a bed rather than to the hard plank of the floor. If one drops a heavy weight on the plank floor, a permanent dent may result. If the weight (within limits) is dropped on the bed, it bounces, and the bed suffers no permanent deformation. Similarly, the carpal bones may be thought of as a series of little box springs or beds that yield under the force applied by the weight of the horse, springing back when the load is removed without suffering a permanent change of shape. In fact, this is a general principle applicable to all bones in the body, but particularly apparent in the knee.

The small carpal bones, then, are acting as spring shock absorbers. They also act, in the overall knee system, as elements in a hydraulic shock absorber. The synovial fluid in the joints between the rows of carpal bones is the hydraulic fluid. The knee, then, combines the spring and hydraulic shock absorbers of the automobile into a single structure. When the force of the horse's body weight is applied to the foreleg, the synovial fluid combines with the elastic articular cartilage and the springy carpal bones to absorb the applied force. As the weight passes over the leg, the energy stored in these three structures is released and the bones and cartilage return to their original shape.

In addition to this shock-absorbing function, the knee must be a completely rigid, immovable joint when bearing full weight and freely movable when not loaded, when the foot is off the ground. These are very demanding mechanical conditions that usually are avoided by the human engineer when he is designing a machine. He prefers to use two parts for these two functions, rather than combining them into a single unit.

The advantages of flexing the leg, primarily at the knee, when protracting the leg have already been discussed. The requirement that the carpus be immovable when the leg is loaded is a bit too complicated for full discussion here. In effect, the locked, immovable carpus contributes to smooth forward motion of the horse's body. In order to achieve the locked position, the radius, cannon, and two rows of carpal bones make complicated rotating movements before the hoof impacts. Briefly, when the carpus is moving, hoof off the ground and the leg protracting, the several joints do not fit together in perfect congruity. As the leg is protracting, they move into positions of greater and greater congruity until they fit together perfectly (locked or "close-packed") before the hoof impacts with the ground.

The clinical signs of damage to the carpus are clear and simple. The horse shows pain when walking, swings the injured limb to the outside to avoid knee flexion, and carries more weight on the normal leg. Often both increased heat and swelling can be detected; in other words, there is inflammation.

This pain and swelling, "popped or sore" knee, is caused by *arthrosis* involving either one or both of two sites within the carpus. Arthrosis is damage to the articular cartilage: erosion and wearing away of the cartilage. It is similar in appearance and cause to what one can accomplish by banging away on a brick with a dull chisel. Once the erosion has appeared, the joint attempts to repair itself. One consequence of this repair effort is the appearance around the margins of the joint of new bone formation, osteophytes (osteo= bone; phyte=plant; a plantlike bony mass). These new bone growths are usually called *calcium deposits* or *spurs*.

Osteophytes are the most obvious changes that one can see on the X-ray film. The cartilage itself is radiolucent, that is, it does not hold up the X-ray beam, and appears clear on the film. Since bone is radiodense, does hold up the X-ray beam, it appears white on the film. As a result, we can see the formation of new bone going on but cannot appreciate the primary erosive changes in the joint cartilage. Once the cartilage is sufficiently destroyed, the clear space between the bone ends narrows, and we know for sure that the cartilage is worn away. This is a subtle change, however, and is best left for the experts to interpret.

The arthrosis occurs either at the lower end of the radius or in the cartilage covering the radial and third carpal bones (Figs. 35–39).

The lesion at the lower end of the radius tends to occur in horses that are over-on-the-knee, while the radial carpal, C 3, lesion tends to occur in animals back-on-the-knee. The first type is, in general, less severe and serious than the second type.

The back-on-the-knee horse is predisposed to developing arthrosis of the radial carpal, C 3, area. A horse that is fatigued, tired at the end of a race, for example, can become *functionally* back-on-the-knee even though he is not built that way. As the muscles on the back of the forearm become tired, they will be less efficient in holding the

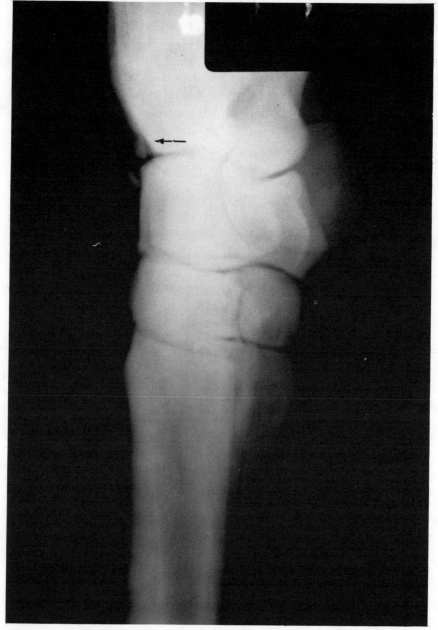

Fig. 35. Radiograph of damage (arrow) to the lower end of the radius.

carpus straight and locked. As a result, the carpus will move backward, further than it should, and we have functional back-on-the-knee.
In a similar manner, fatigue of the muscles on the front of the

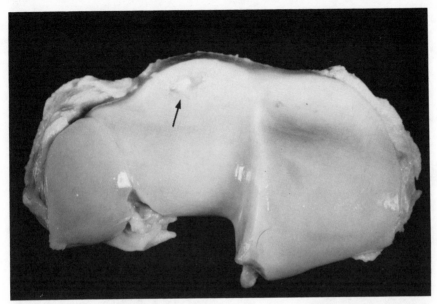

Fig. 36. Postmortem specimen of lower end of the radius showing cartilage erosion (arrow) which corresponds to the damage seen in Fig. 35.

forearm, the extensor carpi radialis in particular, will allow the leg to flex slightly, or remain slightly flexed, when the hoof impacts. This fatigue effect can be exaggerated if the foot is large and heavy (toe weights, horseshoe). Therefore, the animal will be functionally over-on-the-knee. This is an important concept: an animal can be so built that he is predisposed to arthrosis of the carpus or he can become that way because of fatigue.

Fatigue and conformation, then, are two of the major factors that can lead to carpal arthrosis. The horse seems to have been designed as a twenty-to twenty-five-mile-per-hour animal, perhaps thirty when really scared to death. Man has, however, selected for speeds greater than this, up to forty miles per hour and even more. This has led to many problems which we shall detail as we go along. In this specific instance, however, we have a horse capable of running forty miles per hour on a carpus and muscles both designed for twenty-five miles per hour. This great increase in acceleration means more force (since force equals mass multiplied by acceleration), more fatigue, and more articular cartilage damage.

This is as good a place as any to consider the concept of fatigue, which we shall encounter again and again. For our purposes let us say that there are two kinds of fatigue—a great oversimplification!

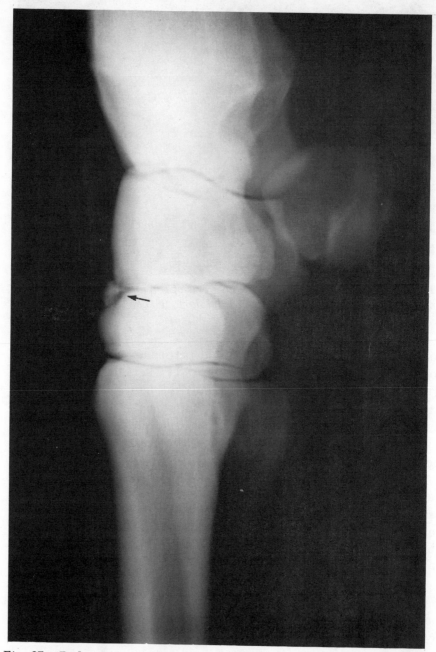

Fig. 37. Radiograph of damage (arrow) to the radial carpal bone and the third carpal bone.

Fig. 38. Postmortem specimen showing marked destruction of joint cartilage of radial and third carpal bones (arrow heads).

The first is the obvious sense of being tired, muscles contracting
slowly or out of phase. The second, and most important here, is a
difficult concept, only partially understood in inanimate materials
and probably not at all in the living organism. Failure of a material
by fatigue occurs when the material is subjected to a series of loadings
or impacts, none of which causes failure individually, but the sum
of which over a period of time does cause failure. A given structure
can safely withstand a given amount of weight if that weight is applied
slowly, statically. It can withstand somewhat less weight applied
dynamically, suddenly. A weight that the structure can support
dynamically, however, if applied repetitively, over and over again,
will eventually cause the structure to fail, collapse. Such repetitive
trauma is common in structures subjected to high speed vibration,

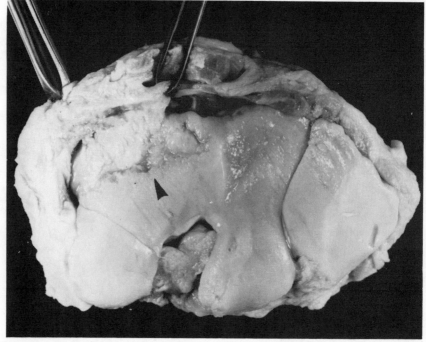

Fig. 39. *Postmortem specimen with severe erosion and some scar tissue healing (arrow) of the third carpal bone.*

such as airplane wings. The wing may move up and down many times, always within the limits of strength of the aluminum. Fatigue can eventually cause failure, however; the wing breaks off.

Fatigue failure of this type appears to be a major factor in the development of arthrosis. Any one blow the cartilage can withstand, but when repeated over and over again, damage will be done.

We race around turns which can be quite short and tight, throwing a greater load on the inside leg. We race horses on hard, dirt tracks, increasing both concussion and fatigue. A very real factor that seems to be increasing in importance is yet another facet of heredity (certainly over-the-knee and back-on-the-knee conformation can be hereditary). We are selecting for high-speed horses as breeding stock, particularly for the precocious two-year-old winners. Some of these fast horses break down with popped knees during their three-year-old year, and having done well as two year olds, are sent to stud duty, "retired due to an unfortunate accident." With certain lines of Thoroughbreds, at least, the unfortunate accident was that they were born with improperly developed carpal bones. To be scientific, they have hypoplasia of the carpus: the bones have not developed to the proper size and/or shape. Needless to say, the great forces exerted at high rates of acceleration are going to be particularly deleterious to a joint that was not properly built to begin with. Some of the most successful stallions of recent times have thrown a number of foals with extremely malformed knees. It is an old saw to breed the best to the best to get the best. Best, however, is not speed and money alone. It is the ability to stand up under training and racing. A two year old that wins a half million, goes like the wind, and breaks down with popped knees as a three year old should be revered, given awards, wept over, and castrated—promptly!

How does one prevent popped knees? Buy horses with strong, well-developed knees from bloodlines with minimum history of the problem. *Train them thoroughly and well* to withstand the fatigue of high-speed, sprint racing. Best of all, start a movement to encourage distance racing at moderate rates of speed rather than sprint racing. The two-dollar bet remains the same, and you only have to wait a minute or two longer to tear up your losing ticket.

A clear illustration: harness horses ten to fifteen years ago were thoroughly trained for gait and stamina. They were raced lightly as two year olds, and the two-minute mile was rare. Today they slap on the hobbles, make everything pace, and push the two year olds. Ten years ago carpal arthrosis was uncommon in harness horses; today it is routine.

As much as I should like to avoid the subject, I have to talk about treatment. You have done everything I have told you not to; so what next? Rest, that's all, rest, cold water, hot water, whatever liniment smells best to you, and careful, gradual return to training when the pain has subsided. I know! Steroids. You are going to inject that knee, aren't you? A single injection of steroid into the damaged carpus after the pain and swelling have subsided followed by prolonged rest is undoubtedly very efficacious. If, however, you inject that carpus and keep going, repeating the injection whenever pain appears, you are eventually going to destroy the joint and the horse. Simply put, steroiding a joint is equivalent to nerving the joint. Steroids slow down or stop the process of inflammation, thereby relieving pain. The horse does not know he hurts and keeps trying for you. Continued working of the damaged joint increases the damage until he becomes a hopeless cripple (Fig. 40). While steroids have their place, they must be used judiciously, for your benefit and for the horse's benefit. The damage I see in the knee at autopsy today as compared to ten years ago is quite astonishing, and a lot of that astonishment is due

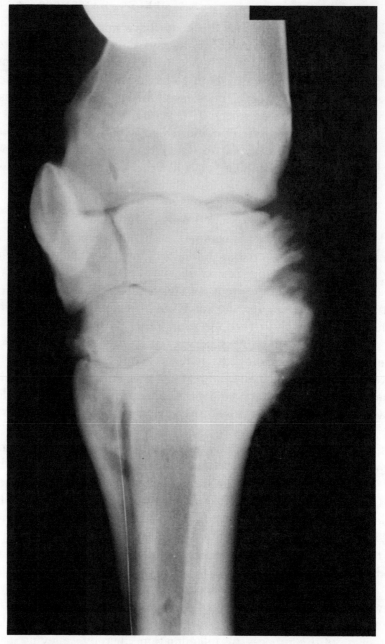

Fig. 40. A carpus severely damaged following steroid injections. There is massive new bone formation (osteophytes).

to improper and continual use of steroids.

Surgical removal of the osteophytes and small chip fractures (which occur as a result of the arthrosis) seems to be successful in returning many knee-sore horses to racing. One of the problems with knee surgery, however, is that we do not really know how well many of these horses may have done with rest and without surgery. I am not aware of any significant study of, say, 100 horses operated on and their subsequent performance as compared to 100 horses with the same type and amount of damage who were not operated on. We spend thousands of dollars on drugs and surgery and nothing on evaluating the efficacy of such drugs and surgery.

I noted, parenthetically, that chip fractures can occur in the knee. As a rule these are quite small pieces of bone that come off the front edge of the carpal bones because the cartilage protection has been destroyed and removed (erosions, arthrosis). Occasionally, one sees a rather large fracture of the third carpal bone (Figs. 41, 42) which may be predisposed to by arthrosis or may occur as a single event fracture. Prompt surgical repair will often return such horses to racing and/or working soundness.

FRACTURE OF THE ACCESSORY CARPAL BONE

The other significant, though much less common, lesion of the carpus is fracture of the accessory carpal bone. In Fig. 43 you can see that there are two forearm muscles that attach to the accessory carpal bone. Interestingly, each of these muscles is innervated by a different nerve: flexor carpi ulnaris by the ulnar nerve and the ulnaris lateralis by the radial nerve. This immediately opens the door for possible loss of synchronization of these two muscles. If we assume that the ulnaris lateralis muscle contracts a split second after the flexor carpi ulnaris at the moment when the weight comes on the leg, the bone should break as shown in Fig. 44. If both muscles contract simultaneously, as they should, the bone will not break. Such loss of muscle synchronization might be expected in the very tired horse, throwing more weight than usual on the leg: the steeplechaser near the end of long run or race, for example. A thousand-pound horse running on the flat can develop as much as 1,500 to 2,000 pounds of force on one foreleg (when that leg is in single support). The jumping horse may well develop forces twice that amount (though there are no direct measurements available).

There may be quite significant inflammation and distension of the carpal sheath with such fractures. This sheath is really a long, narrow bursa that surrounds the superficial and deep flexor tendons behind the carpus. It may, rarely, become inflamed without accessory carpal

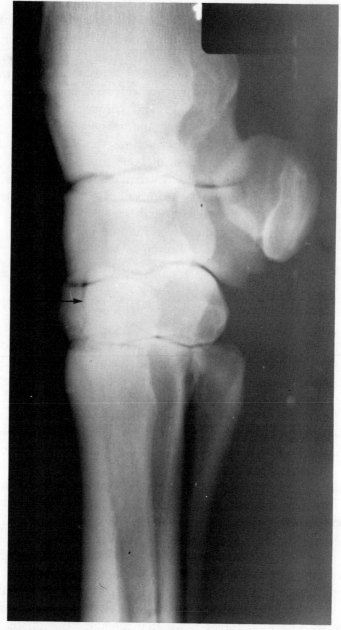

Fig. 41. *Radiograph of a slab fracture of the third carpal bone. The arrow indicates the radiolucent fracture line.*

fracture, but the cause of such inflammation is not clear at the present time.

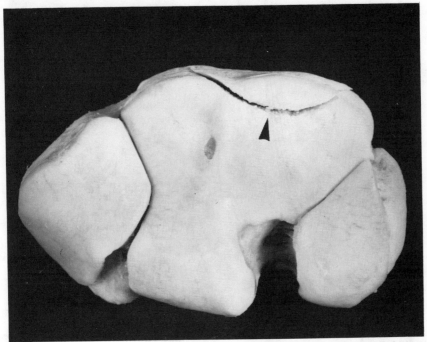

Fig. 42. Postmortem specimen of third carpal bone with a large slab fracture.

Surgical repairs usually are unsuccessful. Most accessory carpal fractures do well if the horse is placed in a cast for one to two months and stall rested for a minimum of six months, and usually up to a year.

SPLINTS

Splints (Figs. 45, 46) are one of the commonest lesions to which the horse is heir; they are, however, of relatively little importance. The horse walks on only one digit as I have already discussed, having disposed of two completely and reduced the other two markedly. What remains of these two reduced digits are the splint bones. In the young horse they are attached to the cannon bone by a thick, heavy ligament called the interosseous ligament (inter=between; osseous=of or pertaining to bone). The acute splint, often called *green* splint, is a tearing of the interosseous ligament with the resulting inflammation appearing as a swollen, hot, painful area in the space between the splint bone and the cannon bone of the front leg. The usual site is the inside of the front leg. (Splints are quite rare in the

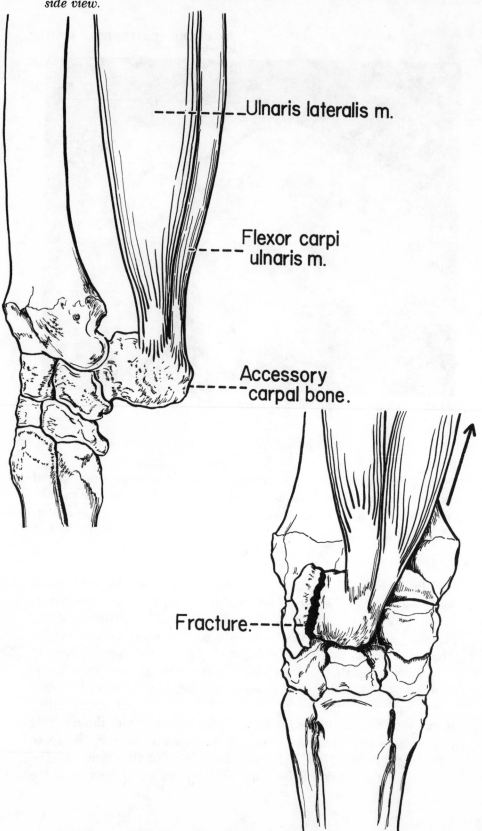

Fig. 43. *The accessory carpal bone and the two muscles that attach to it, side view.*

Ulnaris lateralis m.

Flexor carpi ulnaris m.

Accessory carpal bone.

Fracture.

Fig. 44. *Rear view of carpus. The pull of the flexor carpi ulnaris (arrow) will fracture the accessory carpal bone if the ulnaris lateralis does not contract at the same time.*

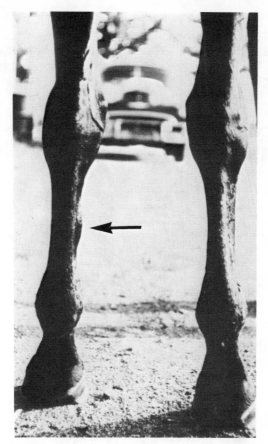

Fig. 45. Splint (arrow) on the inside of the leg.

rear leg and occur on the outside rather than the inside.) Following the acute inflammation associated with the tearing of the interosseous ligament new bone is formed (Fig. 46). Such new bone always forms whenever a ligament is torn away from its attachment to bone.

Why does all this happen? The story is somewhat complicated. The articulation between the inside splint bone of the foreleg and lower row of carpal bones is such that the splint bone is pushed down and back when the leg is loaded. The outside splint bone is only pushed down. Therefore, if the young horse is overworked and/or overloaded before the ligament attains full strength, the inside bone may be pushed in two directions at once and pushed so far that the ligament tears. Interestingly, the arrangement in the rearleg is just the opposite; the outside splint bone is the one that moves in two directions at once. When the new bone forms, it acts as a wedge,

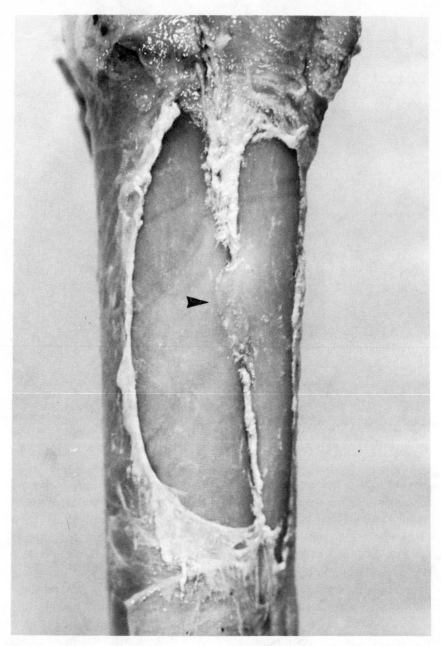

Fig. 46. Postmortem specimen of a splint. The cannon bone is to the left and the splint bone is to the right. The normal, white ligament has been replaced by bone (arrowhead).

holding the splint bone in the loaded position, so that further tearing cannot occur.

A particularly significant and interesting cause of splints has its origin in improper nutrition. If nutritional secondary hyperparathyroidism develops in a young horse, splints are often the first sign. Simply put, hyperparathyroidism means that a horse is on a diet with too much phosphorus in relation to the amount of calcium. This can occur either because of too low calcium in the diet or more commonly because of too much phosphorus. Heavy bran feeding (a phosphorus-rich food) is often associated with this disease. With such a diet the parathyroid gland produces a hormone that causes the removal of calcium from bone to the blood stream in an attempt to maintain the blood levels of calcium at normal levels. It so happens that the first calcium to be removed is in the outer layers of bone, the area where ligaments are attached to the bone. When the calcium is removed from the outer layers, the ligament attachments are loosened and the ligament is more apt to tear away from the bone. Therefore, the interosseous ligament between the splint and cannon bone will tend to tear away more easily when the horse is on a high phosphorus diet. The location of the splint, then, is determined by the mechanics of the splint bones and their articulation with the carpus, but the tearing is predisposed to or set up by the weakening of the ligamentous attachment to the bone.

Let us take a specific example of such a problem. In an area of the country that shall remain nameless, the soil is very rich in limestone, an excellent source of calcium. Every now and then a farm decides the pasture has been around long enough and needs to be torn up, analyzed, and renovated. This sort of thing is aided and abetted by soil people in agricultural colleges, not to mention commercial soil testing laboratories. The soil analysis reveals high calcium and low phosphorus. So, the farm fertilizes heavily with phosphorus, reseeds, and smiles as the new lush grass appears. Obviously, that is now the best pasture on the farm, isn't it? It is not natural anymore, man has improved it, done well by it, changed nature for the better. The farm puts its sales yearlings, the most valuable things on the farm at the moment, on this pasture. Soon thereafter splints begin to pop out like crocuses in the spring. The soil now has too much phosphorus, the grass has too much phosphorus, the horses eat the grass, the parathyroid gland is awakened by the improper calcium-phosphorus ratio, the hormone reabsorbs the calcium from the bone, and the ligaments tear. The result is a splint. The following year the problem does not reappear on that pasture because nature has leached out the excess phosphorus. The soil is back in balance, and the horses do fine.

What do you do about splints? First, check the horse's diet and be sure it is balanced. Take the sack of bran out and pour it on your driveway. If the diet is okay, ask yourself honestly if you are not working this young animal too much and too long. Do you need to lose weight? Perhaps both you and the horse do, in order to lighten the load on those front legs. Does he toe in or out badly? That can predispose to splints. Do you have a favorite paint, wash, or rub? You know, the kind that smells like a rendering plant fallout so it must be good? Rub it on, anywhere, the horse's neck, your dog, the rail fence. The new bone will form, stop movement, and you can go on with your horse. He will have a lump there, but it does no harm. Rest the horse until the acute reaction subsides. Resume work, slowly and carefully.

BUCKED SHINS

This is a very common condition in the young running horse, usually occuring during the earlier stages of heavy training. The first signs of the problem may only be slight heat, swelling, and pain over the front of the middle third of the cannon bone. If work continues, the horse will become quite lame in the affected leg.

There has been much controversy over the years about precisely what constitutes a bucked shin. A widely prevalent idea has been that it is a tearing of the periosteum (peri=around, osteum=bone), a cellular and fibrous sheath that is closely applied to the surface of the bone. As a result of this tear, the reasoning goes, there is bleeding with the formation of a hematoma (hema=blood, oma=tumor, swelling), a pocket of blood between the periosteum and the bone. New bone is then said to form in this pocket of blood, leading to the radiographic picture of Fig. 47. On the basis of our present knowledge this explanation is wrong. Postmortem studies of a few cases of acute bucked shin have shown that the lesion is an incomplete fracture of the cortex of the cannon bone. As a result of this fracture, there is, of course, pain and the formation of new bone, callus, as with any other sort of fracture. I have seen only single fractures, but some veterinarians have reported seeing several at the same time in the same bone.

It is to be noted that routine X-rays at the time the break occurs may not show changes. The fracture is incomplete and rather small, and only a chance X-ray at exactly the appropriate angle can hope

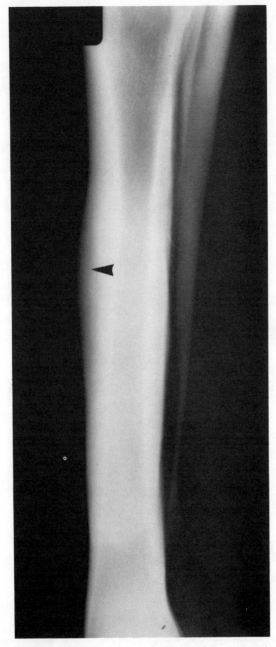

Fig. 47. Radiographic appearance of bucked shin (arrow). Fracture line, which is very narrow, cannot be seen in this view.

to show the fracture line.

The fracture line is, as can be seen in Fig. 48, approximately at an angle of forty-five degrees to the long axis of the cannon bone.

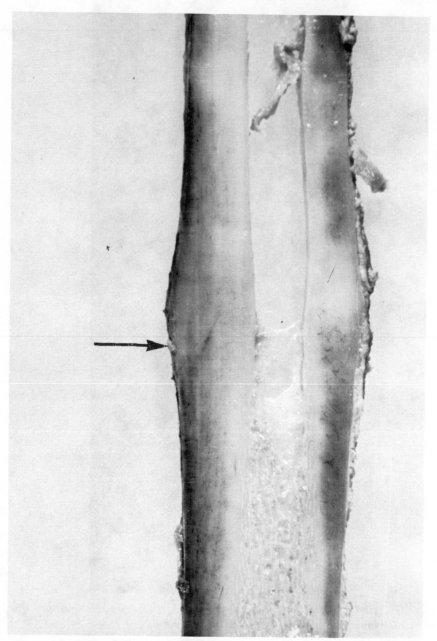

Fig. 48. Postmortem specimen of bucked shin (arrow). Careful examination will show the dark crack in the bone at about forty-five degrees to the long, vertical axis of the bone.

This tells us quite clearly that the fracture occurred because of excessive compression of the bone cortex. When compressed, bone always fails in shear, and shear is always at or near to forty-five-degrees. What is shear? There are three types of deformation that can occur as a result of applying a load to a bone: tension, compression, and shear. If you try to pull a piece of chalk apart, you are putting the chalk under tension. If you press the chalk together between your fingers, it is under compression. At the same time that you are compressing, however, you are generating shear. Keep pressing on the chalk until it breaks and, then, examine the broken ends. You will see that the ends are angulated, at about a forty-five-degree angle to the long axis of the chalk. Shear, therefore, is a force that develops in the bone at a forty-five-degree angle to the compression force.

Why do these fractures occur when and where they do? In the young horse, before heavy training begins, the cannon bone is roughly circular in diameter when cut across. When heavy work begins, the bone starts to remodel, rebuild itself, to meet the new and increased loads put upon it (Fig. 49). This new bone is laid down on the front

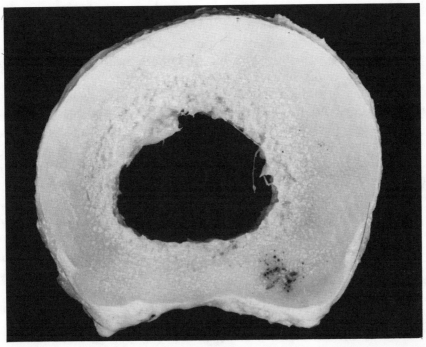

Fig. 49.   Cross section of middle of cannon bone (splint bones removed). The inside of the bone is to the right and is obviously thicker and heavier.

and toward the inside of the cannon. At first this new bone is rather sparse and latticelike. If heavy training continues, a shear fracture may begin in this loose, new bone. If training (loading of the bone) is not excessive, however, the lattice fills in; the bone becomes firm, strong, and able to resist the increased loads.

What do we do to prevent and treat bucked shin? Some perfectly awful things are done. Some trainers say that a horse is shin sore, and the best thing to do is work him hard, "buck him good," blister, steroid, fire. When training the young horse, one should examine the shins (the front of the cannon) carefully after every work. If pain or warmth can be detected, a fracture is beginning. The horse's work should be eased back; breezing should stop. Keep going with the horse but do not push him. We want to keep the animal going so that the bone remodeling process will continue. If we lay him off completely, the fracture will heal, but the remodeling will also stop, and we have to start all over again a month or two later. So, keep him going, but reduce the pace. When the soreness disappears, increase the work again, but ease off once more if pain and soreness reappear in that leg or the other leg. After a variable period, depending upon the individual horse, the bone will have completed its remodeling, and the danger period for bucked shin will be over.

A careful, interested horseman may well be able to follow the course of this remodeling, increase in size of the front, inside part of the cannon, by palpating (feeling) the bone every few days from the time the young animal begins training.

A number of trainers have told me that it does no good to wait to train a horse until he is three or four years old. He will buck then just as well as he will as a two year old. Fair enough. The cannon bone remodels in response to work and load, not age. If that work and load is too rapidly applied to a two year old, he bucks; if not until three, he bucks. It all depends upon careful, deliberate training, not only of the horse as a whole, but of his cannon bone, as well.

I suppose I must mention two forms of therapy that are very popular. A steroid injection will relieve the pain, and the horse will appear sound. Steroids however, inhibit healing. Surely we do not wish to inhibit the healing of a fracture! The firing iron is also popular. It is barbaric and unnecessary and may indeed be harmful. I cannot deny that the iron sometimes seems to help. There is no question about that, but it is acting like a steroid or an injection of novocain. The hot iron burns off and destroys fine nerves to the area so that the horse does not know that he has pain. One must be exceedingly careful about relieving local pain of this sort. It is there for a purpose. It is a feedback that tells the animal something is wrong. When you relieve that pain without correcting the lesion, the horse is liable to damage himself further, to make the initial problem even worse. You cannot tell the horse, as you can a human, to go to bed and rest while that pain is blocked out.

FRACTURE OF THE CANNON BONE

Twisting fractures of the cannon bone occur occasionally. While they are serious, careful splinting and surgical repair may permit at least pasture soundness for the animal. Such fractures in young foals generally have a good prognosis. A number have been repaired with the animal later becoming a useful working proposition. Slab fractures (Figs. 50, 51) are also seen at the lower end of the cannon bone with some frequency. Surgical repair is usually mandatory with this type of fracture (placing screws in the bone) and some horses will return to racing soundness.

FRACTURES OF THE SPLINT BONES

Fractures of the small splint bones are not uncommon, particularly in harness horses. There are three distinct conditions: two true fractures and one pseudofracture. The pseudofracture is a radiolucent line near the lower end of the splint bone that is normally seen in horses up to about two years of age. The splint bone develops from two so-called ossification centers. Some time before birth the splint bone, as most other bones, is made up entirely of cartilage. Blood vessels invade the upper end of the bone, and the cartilage is converted to bone. About three months after birth the lower end of the splint bone is invaded by blood vessels and a second center of bone development (ossification center) begins. If one takes an X-ray between this time and the time the ossification of the bone has been completed (about two years of age), the film will look like Fig. 52. The clear, radiolucent line, indicated by the arrow, is the cartilage still remaining between these two bone-forming centers. One must be very careful, then, about diagnosing a fracture of the splint bone before two years of age.

I must digress briefly here to elaborate about ossification centers since we shall be running into them several times. In early development the bones are first "built" as blocks of cartilage. At different times for different bones, blood vessels invade those blocks of cartilage and, by a complex process, convert the cartilage to bone. Typi-

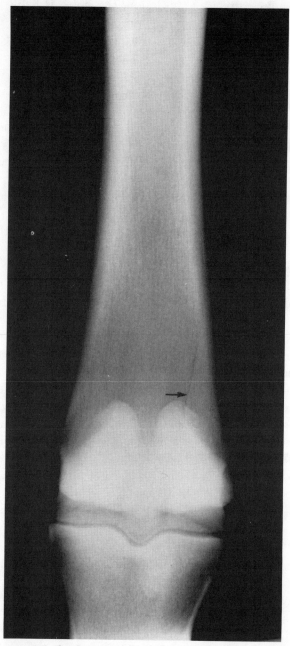

Fig. 50. Fracture of the lower end of the cannon bone (arrow), a radio-lucent line.

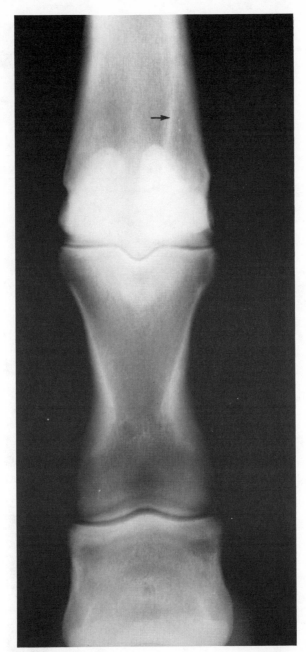

Fig. 51. *Healing fracture of lower end of the cannon bone (arrow), a radiodense line.*

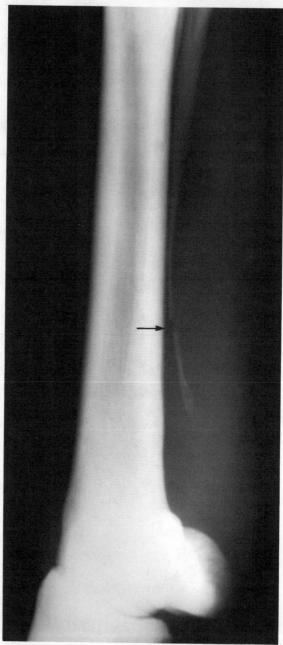

Fig. 52. Normal radiolucent line near lower end of splint bone. One cannot
be certain, on the radiograph alone, in the young horse, if this is or is not
a fracture.

cally the main part of the bone is developed from one ossification center while the two ends are formed by two different centers. Small bones such as the navicular, sesamoids, carpal, and tarsal bones generally form from one ossification center. As we shall see in the appropriate places even these small bones may form from two or more centers (why, we do not know).

The second, true fracture, often simulates a splint since the bone is broken somewhere in the upper third of the splint bone resulting in pain and swelling. Such fractures may be only fine hairline breaks not easily detected on radiographs (Fig. 53). The cause is not completely clear, but may be related to shear fracture because of over-compression of the bone. The treatment is tincture of time, generally four to six months.

The third and probably the most common type is a true fracture of the lower third of the bone (Fig. 54). It should be noted that the clinical signs of fracture may closely simulate those of suspensory ligament "pulls." Radiographs are necessary. We cannot say precisely what causes these fractures but can suggest the following: there is a heavy coating of fascia or connective tissue which runs from the accessory carpal bone of the carpus to the two splint bones (Fig. 55). If the horse's carpus is buckled slightly forward at the moment his foot contacts the ground, it will snap back into the straight position as soon as the load comes on the leg. This snapping will jerk the splint bone as shown in Fig. 56, tending to break it at the lower third. Fractures of the medial splint bone are somewhat more common than of the lateral bone. This is because, mechanically, the pulling force on the medial bone is greater. The pull on the lateral bone is a certain amount, but that on the medial bone will be that amount multiplied by the distance from the accessory carpal bone to the vertical line of the medial splint bone. It is simple mechanics. Similar though somewhat more complicated reasoning applies to fractures of the splint bones of the rearlegs.

There is a greater tendency for animals that pull a load behind them, such as harness horses, to have the carpus slightly buckled forward at the moment of impact of the hoof with the ground. This tendency can be clearly seen in any picture of a draft horse pulling a load (Fig. 57).

The only reasonable approach to treating this problem is surgical removal of the lower fragment of bone. The surgeon may note that if one fractured splint bone is found it is worthwhile to look for others which may, for the moment, be clinically silent but which can cause trouble later on.

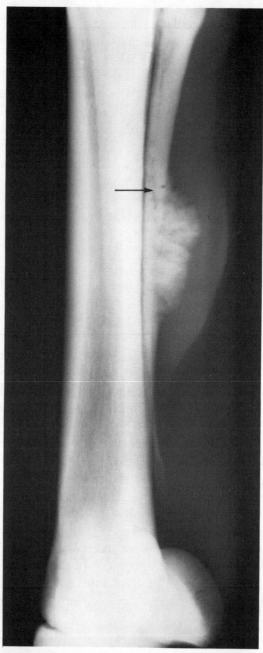

Fig. 53. A hairline fracture (arrow to radiolucent line) of the middle third of the splint bone with exuberant callus formation.

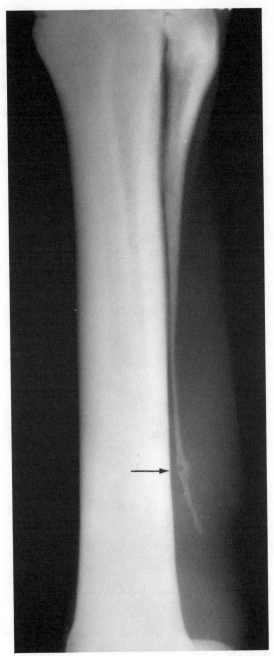

Fig. 54. *This probably is a true fracture because new bone, callus, is present.*

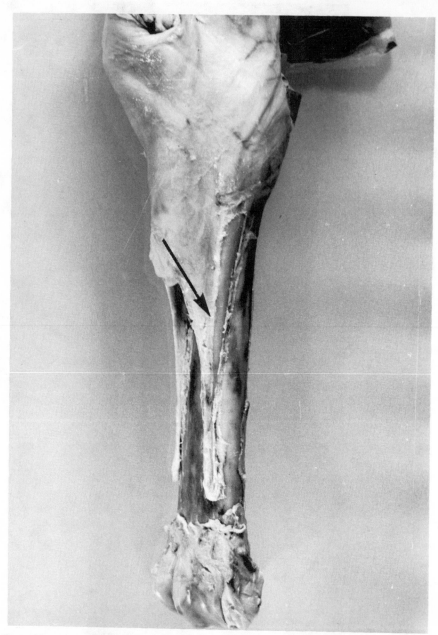

Fig. 55. An oblique rear view of dissected leg showing heavy, white fascia attached to the splint bone (arrow).

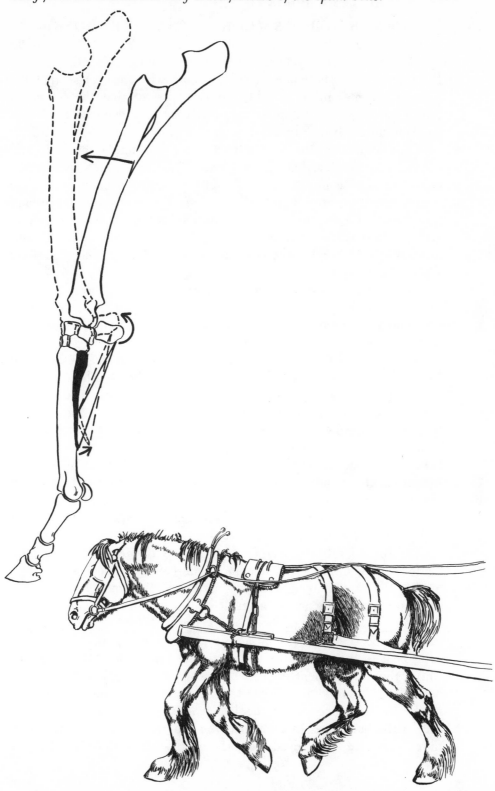

Fig. 56. *Mechanics proposed for splint bone fractures. If the foot impacts with the carpus buckled forward (solid line of radius) and then snaps into proper position (dotted line of radius), the fascia will jerk the splint bone away from the cannon and may cause fracture of the splint bone.*

Fig. 57. *Draft horse under load. The carpus is buckled forward. While this may not be detrimental to the slow-moving draft animal, it could be damaging at racing speeds.*

CONTRACTURES (CONTRACTED TENDONS)

Contractures simply mean that the flexor muscles on the back of the foreleg have shortened (I shall discuss why shortly) so that the pastern becomes more upright, often so upright that the fetlock is buckled forward. In extreme cases the knee may even be fixed in a partially flexed, bent forward, position.

Contractures of the forelimbs are not uncommon in foals and horses, and present difficult problems. There are three established causes of such contractures. Although usually referred to as tendon contracture, the entire muscle-tendon system shortens to pull the limb into an abnormal position. Most contractures involve the forelimb and are flexion contractures. In fact all the muscles, both extensor and flexor, contract, but the flexor muscles are stronger and, therefore, predominate.

The first and least common category is flexion contracture as a result of severe pain in one or more joints. The pain is so great that the muscles contract in an attempt to prevent joint movement and thereby alleviate the pain.

The second category is the most common and affects the newborn foal. The foal is born with contractures of the limbs. There are two subcategories. The first, and more common, is called physiological contracture. During the latter stages of pregnancy the long-limbed foal becomes crowded in the available space within the uterus and, as a result, folds up the legs. Immediately after birth, then, he may be unable to get himself fully "stretched-out." This type of contracture is usually of no significance, and will correct itself within a few hours or days. It is distinctly a waste of time to put casts or other such devices on a foal for several days after birth since he will correct the problem himself if left alone.

The second subcategory of contracture is the result of congenital malformation, improper development, of certain bones in the legs, usually the cannon bone, and the vertebrae, the small bones which make up the backbone. As a result of the malformed cannon bones the joints associated with those bones, primarily the fetlock joint, are unstable and the muscles contract in an attempt to make them stable (Fig. 58). In the case of the vertebrae, the contraction of the muscles causes the development of scoliosis (scolio = curving) or a sideways bending of the backbone (Fig. 59). This bending may not be apparent in the live foal because of the heavy muscles that lie along either side of the backbone. In such foals the prognosis is very poor. Sometimes they are born dead because of dystocia (difficult, delayed

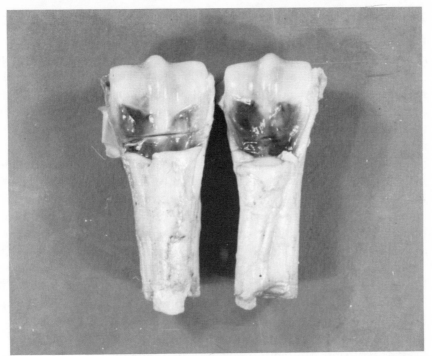

Fig. 58.   The lower ends of the cannon bones from a normal foal (left) and a contracted foal (right). The joint surface of the contracted animal is smaller and less clearly developed than the normal.

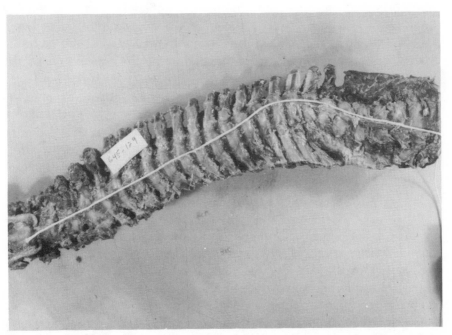

Fig. 59.   Backbone of a contracted foal with scoliosis. Head end is to left and tail to the right. The string emphasizes the curving of the backbone.

foaling). Others are so severely contracted that they cannot stand and have to be destroyed. Casts and other devices are used to straighten the legs of some of these foals, but they probably never become truly useful animals and may contract again when they are yearlings, as will be described below. In most cases, then, this type of contracted foal is a hopeless or useless proposition. Although congenital, the evidence presently available does not suggest that it is hereditary; a mare that has a contracted foal will not necessarily have another.

The third category of limb contracture is that characteristically involving the yearling. There are two subcategories. The first is the animal with malformed bones which was straightened out after birth by casts. This individual may well contract all over again at about a year of age because the bone malformation is still present. The second type of yearling contracture is the sales yearling being fed heavily for sale to someone who will then have to take off all the fat before he can begin serious training. The reason why such individuals may contract is not altogether clear, but it is definitely associated with excessive weight (and not surprisingly, epiphysitis). Many such animals will stop contracting and return completely to normal if put on a diet: no grain, just pasture or grass hay.

At this point we may take up the question of some other types of leg malformation. As mentioned earlier hypoplasia of the carpal bones does occur. If this underdevelopment is sufficiently severe, the leg may be obviously deformed. A common manifestation of this hypoplasia is "knock-knees," resulting from hypoplasia of one or more carpal bones, the lower end of the radius or the upper end of the outside splint bone.

Hypoplasia, if less severe, may not become apparent until the animal grows to a size, usually about a year of age, to put sufficient load on the legs to cause bending. That is, the ligaments may be able to withstand the load of the body up to a certain point, but then they are stretched; there is no bone to carry the load, and the leg deforms.

FETLOCK

The fetlock joint is probably the most frequently damaged joint in the horse's body. This is because it is one of the two joints that normally moves a considerable amount when fully loaded. This point is worth exploring somewhat further. Both the coffin and fetlock joints move to a considerable degree after the weight has come on the leg. Other joints, such as the elbow, stifle, etc. do move, but they do not move as much as the coffin and fetlock.

The coffin joint is rarely damaged because it is very close to the center of rotation for the whole limb, that is, the contact point of the hoof with the ground. The fetlock joint, on the other hand, is the length of the pastern away from the center of rotation. The torque, twisting, or turning, force exerted on a joint is, in part, a function of the distance of the joint from a center of rotation. If a given force is exerted around the coffin joint, the turning force around the fetlock will be multiplied by the length of the pastern. The turning force exerted on the fetlock then is considerably greater than that exerted on the coffin.

The most common lesion of the fetlock joint is the so-called osselet (little bone), like so many other lay terms, a misnomer. The young horse, beginning training, may become lame, developing a soft, hot swelling of the fetlock, particularly on the front. This is known as green osselet. It is in fact an inflammation of the joint capsule of the fetlock as a result of erosion and damage of the articular cartilage on the front edges of the cannon and long pastern bones. There may also be an increase in the amount of synovial fluid within the joint cavity, leading to what is called a wind puff or wind gall. The synovial fluid increases in amount in response to the damage that has been done to the joint cartilage. Whenever a joint is damaged, synovial fluid increases; it is part of the joint's normal reaction to injury.

If the green osselet does not heal, a chronic or cold osselet may develop. That is, the increase in amount of synovial fluid may become permanent, and the thickening and inflammation of the joint capsule over the eroded area persists as a chronic, scarring type of inflammation (Figs. 60–63).

Many horses have this type of damage to one degree or another in their fetlock joints. They may be intermittently sore or lame but often will be serviceably sound for many years once the initial damage has subsided. The situation is summed up in Fig. 64.

A second site of damage is deep within the joint and is not readily detected by any presently available techniques. This is an erosion of the articular surface of the cannon bone near the middle. In the normal bone there is a ridge which serves to separate the front half of the cannon bone joint surface from the back half. When the joint moves, the long pastern articular surface moves on the front part while the sesamoid bones move on the back half. If the fetlock joint moves too far, is overdorsiflexed, the sesamoid bones will be pulled over the ridge. (Dorsiflexion is that movement of the fetlock which makes the angle in front smaller.) The sesamoid bones moving over the ridge is just like driving over a bump in the road at high speed.

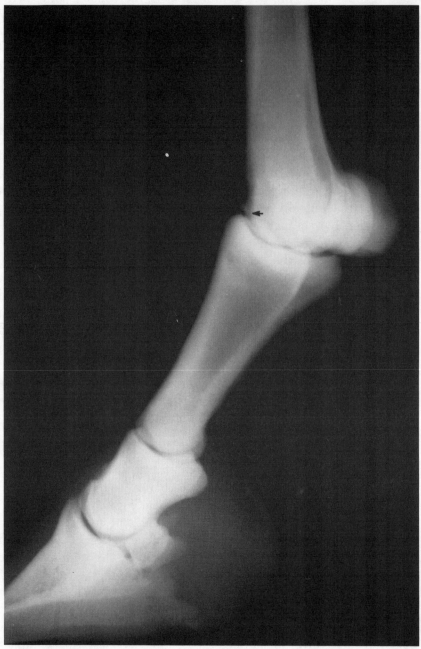

Fig. 60. Radiograph showing new bone formation in the osselet area.

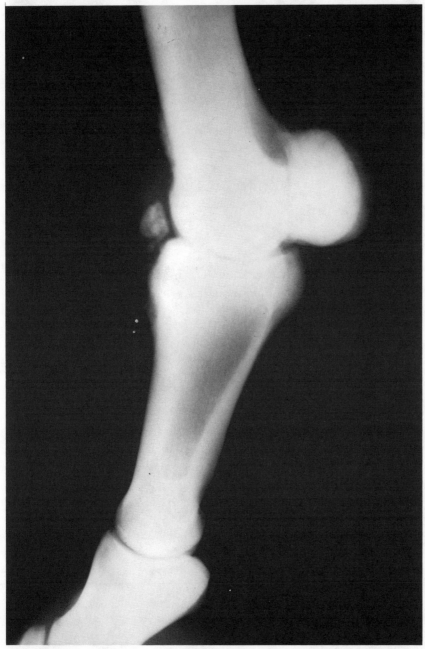

Fig. 61. *More severe example of radiographic changes of osselet.*

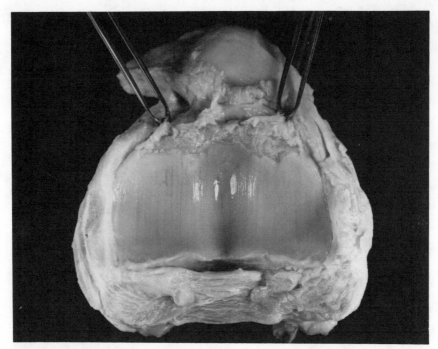

Fig. 62. Upper end of the long pastern bone showing erosions (near the forceps) and wear lines on the articular surface: osselet.

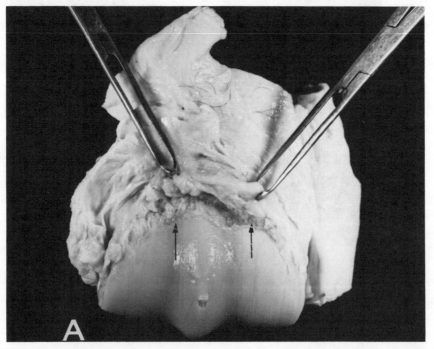

Fig. 63. Erosions of the cannon bone at arrows which are mirror images of those on the long pastern bone of Fig. 62.

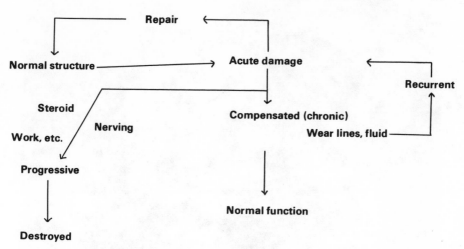

Fig. 64. Mechanism of arthrosis development.

The sesamoid bones get a jolt, and vibrate, causing articular cartilage damage.

Both the "osselet" and the above "ridge lesion" have similar causes. It is simply that the fetlock joint moves too far, dorsiflexes too far, jamming the front surfaces of the cannon and the long pastern together to produce the osselet erosion of the cartilage and, at the same time, pulling the sesamoids over the ridge to produce erosion at that site.

Why does the joint dorsiflex too much? There are several reasons: First, with hard work the animal becomes fatigued, the muscles cannot pull as much and the joint simply keeps moving, beyond its normal limit. Second, we put a weight, ourselves, on his back which increases the total load and hastens fatigue. Third, if the horse has a longish toe and lowish heel, and many are trimmed that way, he will have more trouble raising his pastern during the second half of the stride which will lead to overflexion of the joint. We shall have more to say about that because the long toe, low heel business is associated with a number of other lameness problems in horses as well. A fourth factor is the use of horseshoes, that evil piece of metal which we nail to a horse's foot. The hoof is designed to cut into the ground as one can see by examining the thin, sharp wall of the unshod foot. We place a web of metal over that thin edge and either completely or partially prevent the hoof from cutting into the surface. This causes a precisely similar situation to that of the long toe. Further factors related to the cutting in of the foot will be discussed later.

As a result of the osselet type of arthrosis, osteophytes and small chip fractures of the front edge of the long pastern bone may occur

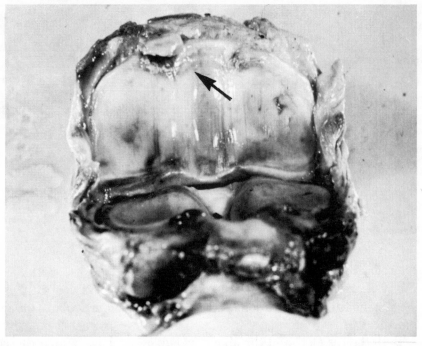

Fig. 65. Chip fracture (arrow) of the front edge of the long pastern bone as a result of osselet damage.

(Fig. 65). Their cause is the same as that already discussed with the carpus. Clinical and surgical experience indicates that the horse is no worse off with this new bone and small fractures than he is with the osselet, per se. Just because one can see them on an X-ray film, then, does not mean that they should be removed. In fact, while removal of such things *may* be good for the carpus, it is definitely not good for the fetlock. It is much better to leave them alone. If the horse is going to become sound again, he will do so just as well with his chip as without it—maybe better.

How do we treat the animal with a sore fetlock? The answer should be obvious. Acute inflammation caused by trauma can be treated with many things. Cold water, hot water, antiphlogistine, oil of wintergreen do no harm. It is perfectly clear, however, that the inflammation will run its course and the lesion heal, as much as it can, only by rest, followed by a very gradual return to full work. Perhaps other modes of therapy are helpful: therapeutic X-ray, diathermy, ultrasonics, but, as of the moment, they have not been evaluated adequately, and one simply cannot recommend any of them as panaceas. Pay attention to the foot. Try to trim the hoof naturally with a reasonable heel and toe. Yes, a horse can sprint faster with a long toe and a low heel, but lameness is the price you pay for that extra bit of speed. Use as narrow a web shoe as possible. Too many horses are too fat; too many people are too fat. Most fetlock arthrosis develops during the earlier stages of training when the horse may still be overweight. An essential prerequisite for training the horse should be dieting. Get him down to a reasonable weight *before* heavy training starts, not during the training period!

PROXIMAL SESAMOIDS

The proximal sesamoid bones are an extremely important component of the fetlock joint and the so-called suspensory apparatus. The major support for the fetlock, pastern, and coffin joints is the suspensory apparatus. This consists of the large suspensory ligament that runs from the back of the carpus to the fetlock (Fig. 66). Just above the fetlock it divides into a number of branches. Two of these branches run around to the front of the pastern and join the common extensor tendon. The great bulk of the suspensory ligament attaches to the upper ends of the two sesamoid bones. Below the sesamoids there are more ligamentous cords which are attached to the base or bottom of the sesamoids and run downward to attach to both the long and short pastern bones. It is clear from Fig. 66 that the entire system acts as a sling to support the fetlock and pastern joints. But why the bones, why not simply a ligamentous system? The sesamoids serve three functions: 1. Bone is stronger than tendon or ligament in resisting compression exerted, for example, by another bone. The downward pressure exerted by the cannon bone is partially received by the sesamoids. If they were not present, the compression load would have to be borne by suspensory tendinous tissue alone and failure would soon result. 2. It is important that the angulation of tendons as they go around joints or insert on bone should be as near constant as possible. That is, the angles should not change as the bones and joints move. We shall investigate this in some detail with the navicular bone. The presence of the proximal sesamoid bones insures that the angles of the superficial and deep flexor tendons will not change as the fetlock moves up and down and rotates on itself. 3. The sesamoid bones move the superficial and deep flexor tendons away from the center of rotation of the fetlock joint. The force which these tendons can exert on the joint, resisting its movement, is, as we have mentioned before, a function of the distance from the center of rotation to the

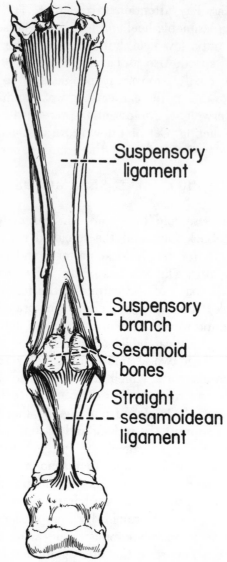

_____Suspensory
ligament

___Suspensory
branch

Sesamoid
bones

Straight
_____ sesamoidean
ligament

Fig. 66. The suspensory apparatus, rear view.

line of action of the tendons. The further the tendons are from the center of the fetlock, then, the greater force they can exert on the fetlock.

There are two major lesions which involve the sesamoid bones, and both of these lesions occur as a result of improper movement of the fetlock joint. As mentioned earlier, the fetlock is a complex joint. The lower end of the cannon bone is composed of two distinct articular surfaces, the one on the front articulating with the long pastern bone

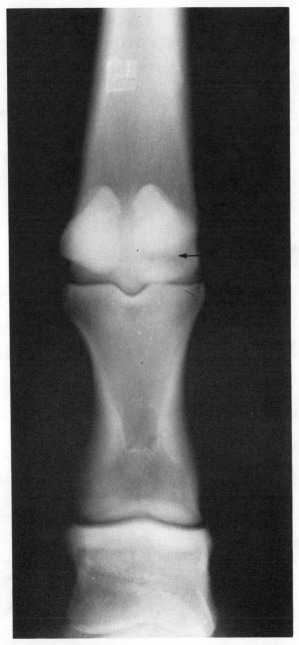

Fig. 67. Radiograph, rear view, of base fracture of the sesamoid bone (arrow.).

and the one on the back articulating with the two sesamoid bones. A definite ridge separates these two surfaces of the cannon bone. When the fetlock joint dorsiflexes too much, as discussed earlier, the

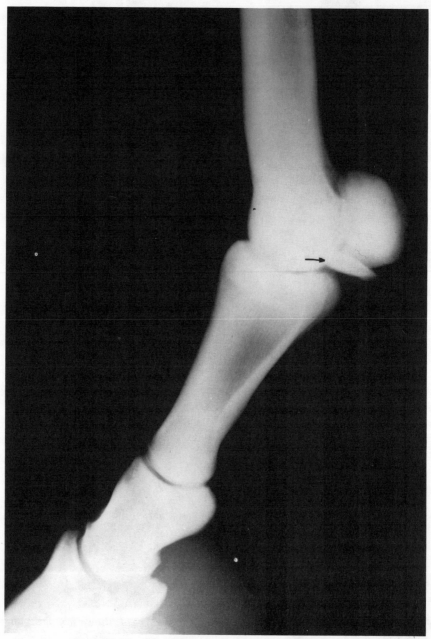

Fig. 68. Radiograph, side view, of base fracture of a sesamoid bone.

sesamoid bones can be pulled over the ridge. If pulled over fast enough and hard enough, the ridge acts as a fulcrum, and the sesamoid bone may be broken near its base (Figs. 67–70). This occurs, as a rule, because the leg is moving too fast relative to the speed of the body, a concept that we cannot go into in detail here. In effect, it occurs most commonly on sharp turns when the outside leg is moving faster than the inside leg in order to "bend" the horse around the turn.

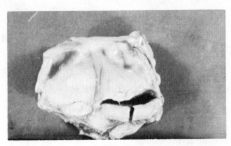

Fig. 69.   Postmortem specimen of base fractures of both sesamoid bones.

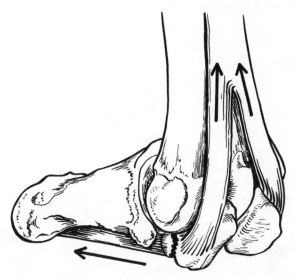

Fig. 70.   Oblique rear view of base fracture of sesamoid.

This type of fracture, so-called base or basal fracture, is more common in Thoroughbreds, and in the United States, at least, is more common in the inside bone of the right foreleg. That is reasonable, as a moment's reflection will show, because we race counterclockwise around turns. In Australia, interestingly, it is more common in the inside bone of the left foreleg, because they go into a turn very gradually and come out of the turn sharply. Such fractures are extremely uncommon in England and Ireland where they do not race around turns or only around very long, dog-leg turns.

The second type of fracture occurs most commonly in harness horses and most frequently involves an apex fracture of the outside bone of the left rearleg (Figs. 71–74). This fracture occurs because the leg is moving too slowly relative to the body. The bone is broken over the ridge at the upper back limit of the cannon articular surface because the sesamoids are pulled *up* too fast. (With the base fracture they were pulled *down* too fast.) Once again, a moment's reflection will show that the inside legs tend to move slower going around a counterclockwise turn, for the same reason that the outside legs move faster. So, sesamoid fractures appear to be largely a function of going around turns.

In both cases the site of fracture, base or apex, and the leg involved are a function of turns. Which of the two bones will break is determined by the normal anatomy and movements of the bones. The outside bone of the rearleg breaks more than the inside bone because it is somewhat taller and cannot clear the upper ridge as fast. The inside bone of the foreleg breaks because it is pulled further over the other ridge when the joint dorsiflexes too much (Fig. 75). This, in turn, is caused by the fact that the fetlock joint rotates on itself (inside to outside) as well as flexing, from medial to lateral (inside to outside), so that the medial sesamoid bone moves farther than the lateral sesamoid bone.

The proximal sesamoid bones normally form from a single ossification center, but, rarely, one sees one that has formed from two centers. A line may show on the radiograph, suggesting fracture.

The second type of sesamoid lesion is so-called sesamoiditis. This, again, is the result of the sesamoid bones being pulled too far when the fetlock joint dorsiflexes. The attachments of the several ligaments to the sesamoid bones are strained or partially pulled loose from the bones. Severe lameness and pain results and, eventually, the formation of new bone, osteophytes (Figs. 76, 77).

How can the same thing, overdorsiflexion of the fetlock, cause all these different lesions? Moderate degrees of over flexion cause osselet and ridge lesions, more severe overflexion causes sesamoiditis. If the flexion is sudden, exaggerated for a very brief period of time, fractures of the sesamoid bones occur. The different lesions, then, are related to how much flexion and how fast; quantitative rather than qualitative.

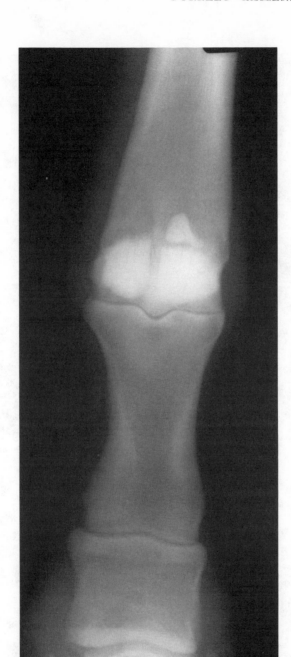

Fig. 71. Radiograph, rear view, of apex fracture of sesamoid bone.

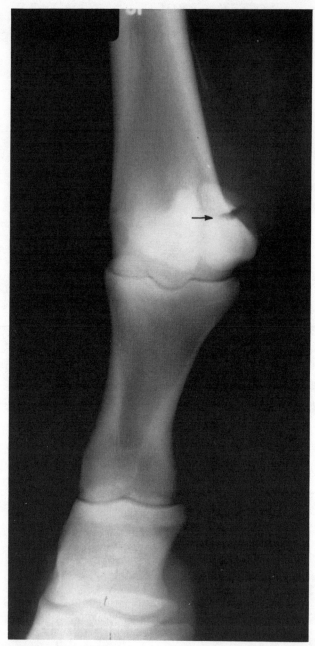

Fig. 72. Radiograph, oblique view, of apex fracture of sesamoid bone.

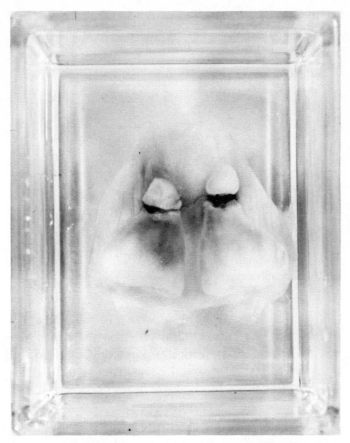

Fig. 73.   *Postmortem photograph of apex fractures of both sesamoid bones.*

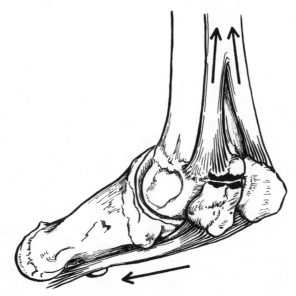

Fig. 74.   *Oblique rear view of apex fracture of sesamoid.*

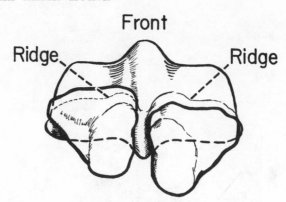

Fig. 75. End on view showing medial sesamoid bone, to the left, pulled over ridge on cannon bone before lateral sesamoid. This is the reason that base fractures of the medial sesamoid bone are more common than base fractures of the lateral sesamoid bone.

With both fracture and sesamoiditis the onset of lameness is sudden and severe, and there may be quite marked swelling over the back part of the fetlock. The area may be exquisitely sensitive to pressure with the fingers. Radiographs show the fractures very nicely. If taken early they may not show any changes with sesamoiditis. Often the new bone formation occurring as a result of the acute tearing of the ligaments may not show up on the X-ray film for a week or more after the initial tearing.

What do you do? Well, first of all, cry a lot. Apex fractures can be handled surgically quite nicely by simply removing the small fractured piece of bone. Many of these horses go back to training and do fine. Base fractures are much less successfully handled, surgically or any other way, and few of those animals can return to serious training. These fractures simply do not heal well by bony union because it is nearly impossible to completely immobilize the fetlock and coffin joints, and the constant movement prevents bony union. At best one gets fibrous union, union with scar tissue, and that is not strong enough to withstand the loads of heavy training. If casting is to be attempted, the entire digit, fetlock to ground, must be immobilized because movement of the coffin joint is just as bad for sesamoid healing as movement of the fetlock. The suspensory apparatus is the main supporting structure for the whole digit, and movement of any joint of the digit, fetlock, coffin, or pastern will cause movement of the suspensory apparatus, and the sesamoid bones are part of that apparatus.

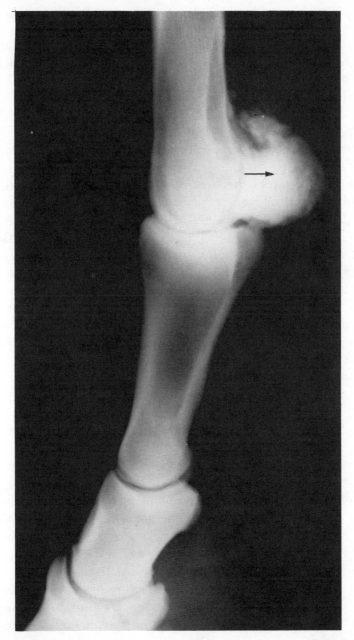

Fig. 76. *Radiograph of severe sesamoiditis with new bone formation and destruction of the normal bone structure.*

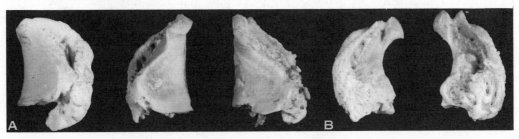

Fig. 77. *Osteophytes as a result of sesamoiditis, postmortem specimens.*

Sesamoiditis is a very bad lesion. Very rarely does a horse with true, full-blown sesamoiditis ever return to full work. Somewhat lesser degrees of damage, if the horse is rested long and well, and his feet trimmed properly, may allow return to full or nearly full work.

It is clear, then, that the best recourse for these sesamoid lesions is to prevent them as far as possible. We can only do that by trying to prevent overdorsiflexion of the fetlock. We can only do *that* by *not* trimming the hoof to the low heel, long toe shape. Keep the toe reasonably short and the heel reasonably high: the way the horse wears his hoof if allowed to go barefoot without human intervention. We can also reduce the weight of both horse and rider. Sharp turns, clearly, should be avoided. No, I do not know how you do that, given our present-day tracks! (But see chapter 6.) Perhaps some track architect will read and heed, however. Many tracks are banked in the turns, but they are usually banked by eye and by gosh, not by science. It is possible to determine how a turn should be banked; it is done for human foot, car, and motorcycle racing, and it could be done for the horse as well if anyone would take the time, make the effort, and expend the money.

About firing, blistering, rubs, etc., obviously they are worthless here as almost everywhere else.

THE LONG PASTERN BONE (PHALANX I)

The major problem with this bone is the so-called screwdriver fracture (Figs. 78, 79). The configuration of the fracture lines allows us to clearly define the cause. As mentioned above, the fetlock joint rotates on itself at the same time as it flexes and extends. When the horse is elevating the pastern during the second half of the stride, pushing with the foreleg, the long pastern bone is rotating from lateral back to medial (outside to inside). If this rotation is accelerated by the hoof slipping back, a fracture may occur. Rarely, one sees a horse that slips forward. In this case, fracture can also occur but will be the exact opposite, mirror image, of the fracture associated with slipping back.

This type of fracture occurs on slippery, wet going. It is quite common in England where they work and race on grass and, to put it mildly, it rains a lot.

In Newmarket, England, one of the favorite gallops is a lovely stretch of heath called the Limekilns because the soil is of a porous, rapidly drying limestone type. The veterinary surgeons there know that, after a dry spell, followed by a light evening rain, horses will

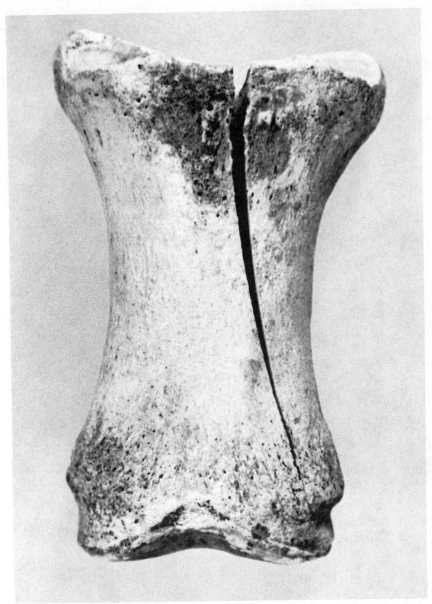

Fig. 78. So-called screwdriver fracture of the long pastern bone.

often fracture long pastern bones at a great rate. The limestone soil dries out quickly; the light rain moistens the long grass, and a perfect slippery surface is created: the hoof cannot cut into the dry ground sufficiently and slips on the grass instead. Add to this the rolling, uphill nature of parts of the gallop, and pastern fractures become a

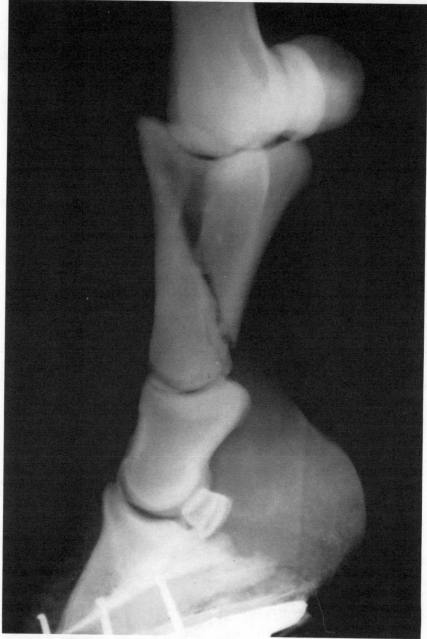

Fig. 79. Radiograph of severe screwdriver fracture.

way of life. Once again, the horseshoe contributes because it tends
to prevent the foot cutting into the ground, adding to the risk of
slipping. I remember, years ago, a harness horse trainer who loved

muddy, wet tracks. He was a blacksmith and whenever it rained, he pulled the shoes from any horses he had going that night. If ever there was a sure bet, his horses were sure bets on muddy tracks. Naturally, they got much better traction because the foot, without metal, could cut into the soft going.

In the United States such screwdriver fractures are probably seen most often in cutting, roping, barrel racing horses. Large caulks may be put on the shoes of such animals, and when they make those sharp, low, sit-down turns the foot is riveted to the ground, the body twists around, and the pastern is broken.

How to prevent? I am sure it is clear: do not use your horse on slippery going and, if you must, pull the shoes. One can easily lower the incidence of pastern fractures in stock horses by avoiding heel caulks.

Repair of such fractures, if not excessively comminuted and smashed, can be accomplished by casting and, in some cases, surgical plating and screwing.

Similar fractures of the short pastern bone do occur (Fig. 80) (generally in Quarter Horses) but, in my experience, at least, are much less common than those of the long pastern. Casting is probably the only recourse once the fracture has occurred, because of the bone's partial location within the confines of the hoof.

RINGBONE

It is somewhat difficult to define this condition because almost any new bone formation felt or seen anywhere between the fetlock and hoof is called ringbone. So I shall begin by defining. There are two types of ringbone: articular and nonarticular. The terms high and low ringbone are often used. High ringbone is new bone formation around the pastern joint and low ringbone is new bone around the coffin joint. The former is much more common and is the type I am discussing here, as low ringbone is rarely a sole reason for lameness.

Articular ringbone is an arthrosis of the pastern joint (Figs. 81–84). As a result of the arthrosis, osteophytes form around the pastern joint. Often such osteophytes can be felt, and they are easily visible on a radiograph. The arthrosis develops as a result of pastern joint over-dorsiflexion. This type of lesion develops most often in high-speed horses, hunters, and working Quarter Horses. A clear example, however, was defined by the careful Norwegian worker, Haakenstad, in a breed of Norwegian draft horses. These animals developed pastern arthrosis and ringbone at an early age. He showed that the

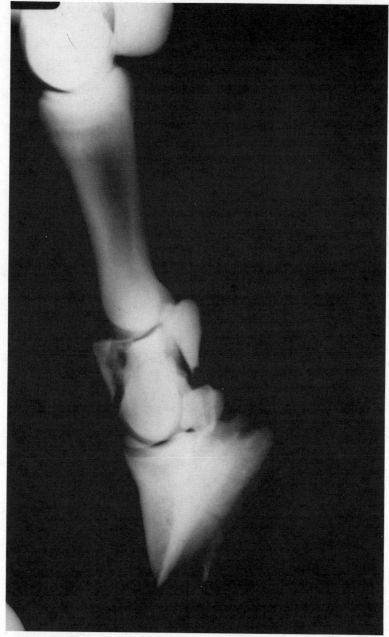

Fig. 80. Severe fracture of short pastern bone.

ridge on the short pastern bone, which helps to resist the rotatory movement of the joint, was underdeveloped (hypoplastic) as a genetic condition, in this breed. As a result, even relatively slow speed move-

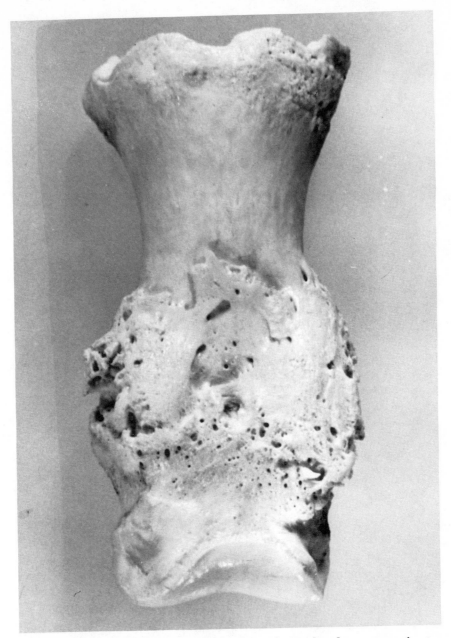

Fig. 81. Long and short pastern bones fused together by a mass of osteophytes: ringbone.

ment allowed the long pastern bone to rotate too far on the short pastern bone, putting excessive pressure on one part of the joint with consequent cartilage destruction and arthrosis.

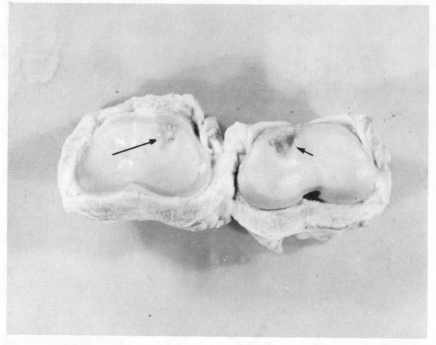

Fig. 82. *Erosions of the lower end of the long pastern bone (arrow to the right) and coincident surface of the short pastern bone (arrow to the left): articular ringbone.*

The second type of ringbone is nonarticular; that is, new bone forms in the pastern area without the presence of pastern joint arthrosis. This new bone may form in any one of a number of sites. This is because this new bone is forming in response to tearing of ligament attachments to bone and, obviously, which ligament is torn determines where the new bone will appear. One of the more common types is osteophytes developing in the attachment of the straight sesamoid ligament to the complementary fibrocartilage on the back of the short pastern bone (Fig. 85). This cartilage is an extension of the joint surface of the short pastern bone. With low heels the pastern tends to elevate, become more upright. When it has become more upright, it will move through a wider angular distance when the load comes on the leg. Greater angular distance means greater acceleration and, since force equals mass times acceleration, the force will be greater: ergo, a tendency to tear loose the attachment of the straight sesamoid ligament. When loaded the pastern joint should, normally, dorsiflex, and this dorsiflexion is resisted primarily, though not entirely,

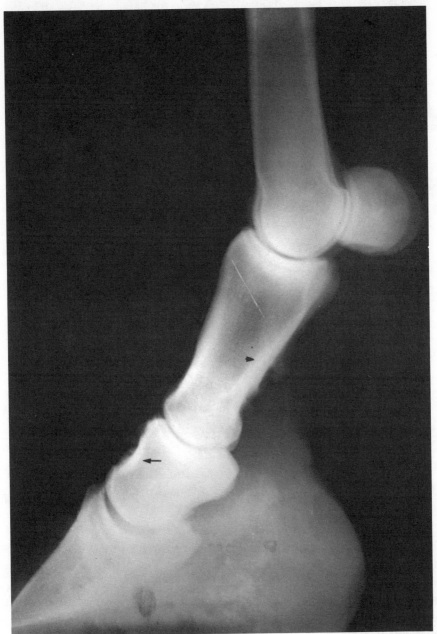

Fig. 83. Radiograph of moderate ringbone. New bone formation at arrows.

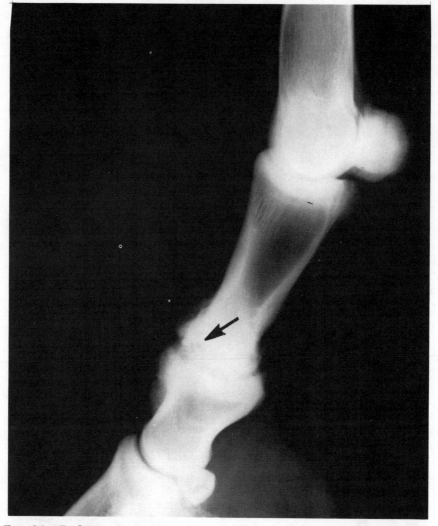

Fig. 84. Radiograph of severe fusion of the pastern joint as a result of articular ringbone.

by this straight ligament. Greater rotatory force exerted during dorsiflexion, then, puts greater strain on the ligament.

Interestingly, such straining of the ligament may result in lengthening of the ligament, decreasing its ability to prevent the pastern dorsiflexion. The final result may then be: strain of the ligament, nonarticular ringbone developing at the attachment of the ligament to the short pastern bone fibrocartilage, decreased resistance to dorsiflexion, which finally leads to articular ringbone. Isn't that a pretty story, and all because the heels are too low!

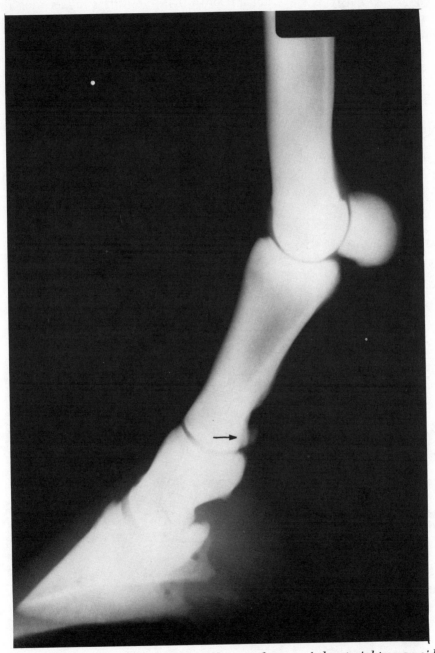

Fig. 85. *Osteophyte developing in the attachment of the straight sesamoid ligament to the complementary fibrocartilage of the short pastern bone.*

Tearing of other ligaments in the pastern area may also be seen. Quite obviously, if one trims a hoof so that one wall is higher than the other, ligaments can be put under excessive strain. It may not be the ligament that appears to be strained as you look at the horse, however. It may well be on the opposite side, because of "snapping" of the ligament as the unbalanced foot contacts the ground and the load comes on the leg (Fig. 86).

Animals with coarse, boxy pasterns are somewhat more predisposed to nonarticular ringbone. This is because the ligaments are further from the center of rotation of the joints, the moment arm is longer, and therefore the force applied to the ligaments is greater.

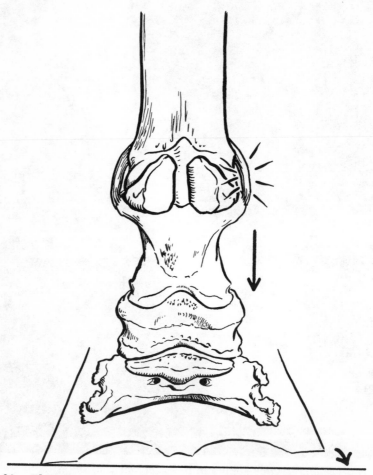

Fig. 86. This illustrates how a ligament at the fetlock could be snapped and damaged if the foot is unbalanced, landing on one side first and, then, snapping down on the ground (lower, curved arrow).

Nonarticular ringbone was certainly common in draft horses, and this is one of the reasons. Another reason is that the big platter foot of those animals was often unbalanced, and they had to work on rough, uneven ground or cobblestones, pulling heavy loads behind them.

There is no real cure for ringbone, articular or otherwise, and that's a fact. What one does is to get the foot back into proper perspective and alignment. This, however, is not always easy to accomplish. Many people complain, with complte justification, about the paucity of good horseshoers and how they cannot get done what needs to be done, if they knew what that was! All true; sad but true. You do have one very neat recourse, however. If you will pull off the shoes and go on with earlier stages of light training, the horse will tell you how his foot should be. Just touch up the edges of the hoof wall lightly with a rasp every so often, pick out the hoof, and let the animal wear himself into the proper alignment. It is obvious that this "natural" approach will not result in the Tennessee walker monster foot nor that of the gaited horse; thus my objection to that type of foot. Horses that have poor conformation for one reason or another may require something different, something not achieved by natural wearing, if they are to do what you want. (It is all right for him, the natural wear, but it may not be for your purposes, nefarious as they are!)

Once the ringbone is with you, it will always be with you, but good trimming and/or shoeing will often add some years to the working life of the animal.

THE FOOT

I define the foot as including all those structures from the coronary band to the ground. The horse has only one "toe." As already noted two of the original five toes have disappeared during evolution while two more have been reduced to splint bones with no toe attached. Rarely we see a foal that is a "throw-back," developing a small, rudimentary toe on the end of one of the splint bones. Such animals look a bit strange, but they can function normally. Our fingernail is the horse's hoof, but, obviously, the horse has elaborated it and made it a great deal stronger for the job that it must perform.

Perhaps we can understand the structure of the horse's foot best by describing what it does while the horse is running: As the foot swings back to contact the ground, the heel normally impacts slightly before the toe, and the relatively thin quarters expand outward. At the same time the short pastern bone is rotating down and back against the digital cushion. The cushion expands outward, pressing against the lateral cartilages, further spreading the quarters. It is often assumed that the frog contacts the ground immediately, pressing upward against the digital cushion (so-called frog pressure). It is more reasonable that the short pastern bone presses the cushion down against the frog, and that the frog touches the ground secondarily, if at all. The soft, normal frog would appear to be poorly adapted for taking the immediate shock of impact. If one examines a section of the foot, it can be seen that the frog and bar can be compared to a complex leaf spring that absorbs impact energy (Fig. 93). It bends down and tends to straighten as the digital cushion is driven down on it by the rotating short pastern bone.

Following heel contact, the toe comes down, and a direct compressive force is exerted upward through the mulitple horn tubules that make up the wall of the hoof. These horn tubules (Fig. 87) are built in a springlike spiral pattern admirably adapted to yield with and absorb the compressive force.

The hoof wall is connected to the coffin bone through an interlocking of the insensitive laminae of the horn wall with the sensitive laminae attached to the coffin bone. The coffin bone "hangs" in laminar "slings" inside the hoof (Fig. 88).

The structure of the coffin bone closely parallels its function and the forces applied to it. If a model is constructed of sticks and pressed on a slippery surface (Fig. 89), the shape of the coffin bone appears.

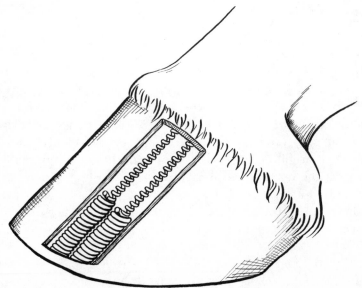

Fig. 87. Schematic representation of horn tubules as elastic springs.

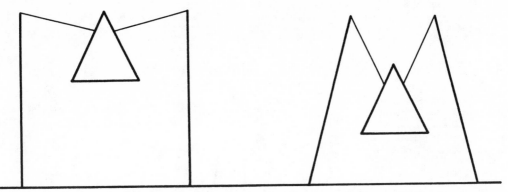

Fig. 88. *Coffin bone (triangle) supported in laminar slings inside the hoof walls. To the left, unloaded and to the right, loaded.*

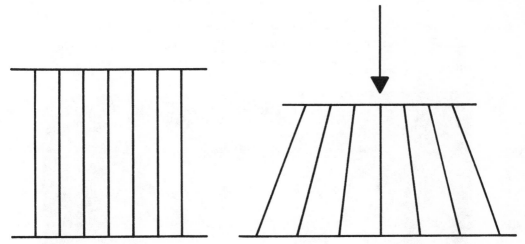

Fig. 89. *Model of coffin bone. To the left a series of sticks. When pressed down, as under normal loading, the sticks move to the positions at the right which is the shape of the coffin bone.*

It is apparent that the coffin bone must be designed to resist tension, rather than, as one may have thought, compression. In our first model, in order to prevent the sticks from separating, cross-braces would have to be provided (Fig. 90). Careful examination of the coffin bone itself (Fig. 91) shows that it has a structure remarkably reminiscent of the models we have developed. The model is not a perfect representation but, in theory at least, with more detailed study, could be brought closer and closer to the real thing. This is, of course, true of all models.

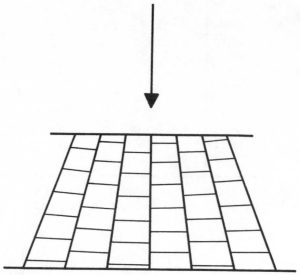

Fig. 90. Cross braces included in the model of Fig. 89 to resist tendency of the sticks to move too far outward.

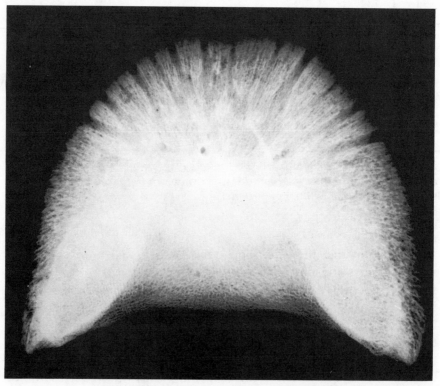

Fig. 91. Radiograph of the coffin bone.

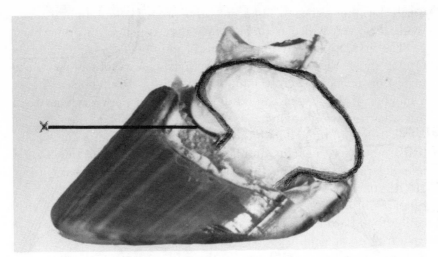

Fig. 92. Dissected foot showing the lateral cartilage. X indicates the coffin joint.

Roughly, then, the hoof wall absorbs the upward force from the ground while the frog, digital cushion, coffin bone, and laminae absorb the downward force of the body, and the total equals zero if all is working properly.

The function of the lateral cartilages is not completely clear (Fig. 92). Since there is an inordinately rich plexus of veins on both sides of the cartilage with numerous interconnections through the cartilage, it may be suggested that the cartilage is a pressure-relief plate. Blood in the axial plexus (the veins in the digital cushion) is heated and moved outward by the pressure exerted on the cushion, shunting through the cartilage in the interconnecting veins to the plexus between the cartilage and the hoof wall. This is probably an important part of the shock absorbing mechanism. The force applied to the cushion compresses the cushion. Some of the energy is dissipated as heat. The heat is "picked up" by the blood in the veins. The blood is moved away from the cushion and, subsequently, up the leg, dissipating energy as heat. This is quite comparable to the radiator cooling system of a car. The pressure developed in the cushion, however, is great enough to shut down the veins, stopping blood flow and, consequently, heat dissipation. By having the veins pass through the relatively rigid lateral cartilage, the venous shunts from the cushion to the outside would be protected from such shut down (Fig. 93).

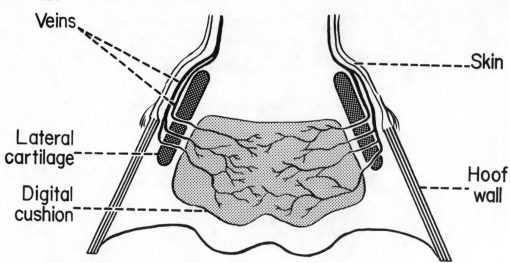

Fig. 93. *Diagram showing venous flow path from digital cushion through lateral cartilages. See text for details.*

The laminae, the slings between the coffin bone and the hoof wall, will be considered next. Once the foot is in contact with the ground, forces are being exerted on the foot as shown in Fig. 94. The details of this are rather complicated and need not detain us. The important two forces are the heavy arrows. The sensitive and insensitive laminae of the foot parallel these forces, a very sensible mechanical arrangement. The reason is shown in Fig. 95. Since the forces tend to distort as from a. to b., the laminae are built as in c.

I should now like to emphasize what I consider to be a very important point that has been alluded to several times previously. The horse's hoof is designed to cut into the ground whenever the animal is exerting any significant force. All one has to do to verify this point is to ride a barefoot horse over reasonable ground and, then, look at the ground. You will see that the hoof has cut in. Now shoe the horse and repeat. Compare the tracks. The shod foot cannot cut in as much because the web of the shoe is wider than the normal, rather sharp bearing edge of the hoof wall. In Fig. 96 we see that as the foot cuts into the ground the distance R decreases to R'. This means that the resistance of the ground to the movement of the hoof is decreasing until, eventually, the resistance becomes zero and the hoof comes out of the ground, at the end of the stride. In Fig. 97 we see what happens if the hoof cannot cut into the ground. The resistance will decrease in the same way, but, in order to do so, the hoof must be raised up, which lifts the whole body weight of the horse,

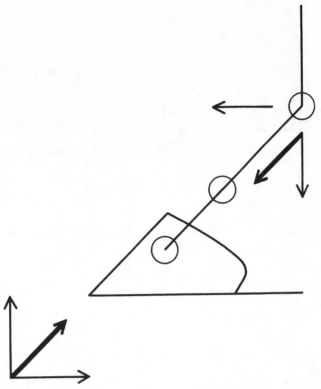

Fig. 94. The forces exerted on the foot. The two heavy arrows are the primary forces and parallel the construction and orientation of the laminae.

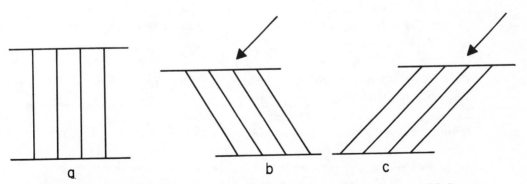

Fig. 95. Orientation of laminae. Since force exerted as in b would distort laminae as from a to b, the laminae are built parallel to the force, as in c, in order to obviate distortion.

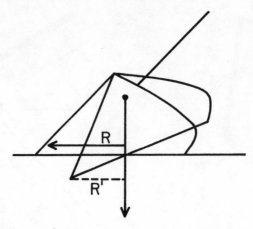

Fig. 96. Diagram of hoof cutting into the ground. See text for details.

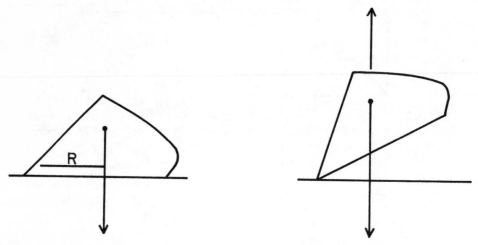

Fig. 97. Diagram of hoof not cutting into the ground. See text.

a very wasteful and fatiguing process. Further, the foot in Fig. 97 will be much more unstable, tending to rock from side to side, than the one digging in as in Fig. 96. One more mechanical point: In Fig. 98 we have a comparison of the angulation of the fetlock when the hoof digs in, a., and doesn't dig in, b. It is obvious that if the foot digs in, the fetlock angle, in front, will not be as small as when the foot does not dig in. This is tricky; study it. You will remember that we said that this small fetlock angle, overdorsiflexion, is the immediate cause of osselet, ridge erosions, sesamoiditis, and sesamoid fracture. We shall

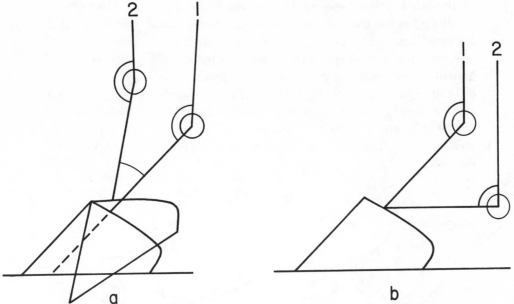

Fig. 98. *a. Hoof cutting into the ground allows full movement without excessive dorsiflexion of the fetlock joint. b. If the foot cannot cut in, the dorsiflexion of the fetlock is excessive (angle becomes very small).*

soon talk about how this angle relates to bowed tendon. I think my point is clear. Horseshoes and/or hard-going (like most racetracks), which prevent the hoof from cutting into the surface, are singularly important factors in a variety of lower leg lameness of the horse.

A nice example of benighted horseshoeing is the case of a French trotter that was a great success in his own country before being purchased for American exploitation. A big name American trainer worked the horse and saw that he paddled in front rather markedly. That would not do! The trainer went to the smith and told him to trim the horse not to paddle, to lower the inside of the toe. The horse did not paddle anymore, but he was so ankle sore from the new alignment of his digit that he could not go a half mile without breaking. When he was finally allowed to go back to his natural paddling (he was a toed-in horse, what else should he do?), he became a racing proposition once more. If you do not want paddlers, do not buy toed-in horses.

NAVICULAR DISEASE

There has probably been more written and said about this little bone than anything else in the horse's body. First, its function: as mentioned with the proximal sesamoid bones (and this is a *distal* sesamoid bone) the major function is to maintain a constant angle of insertion for the deep flexor tendon. Fig. 99 shows what would happen if the navicular bone were not present. The angle of insertion on the coffin bone changes markedly as the bones move. Large changes in angle of insertion may be extremely destructive. It is such changes in angle with the snapping of the ligaments around the pastern joint that leads to tearing and nonarticular ringbone, for example.

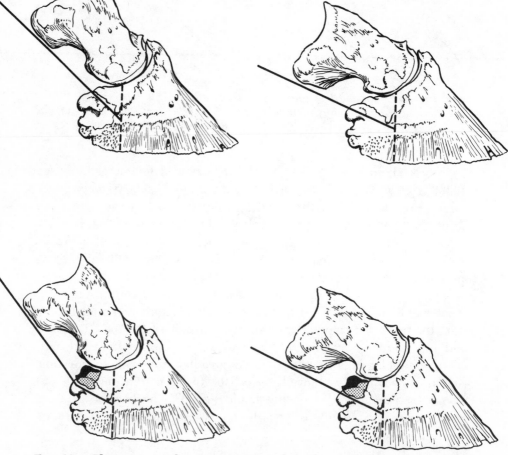

Fig. 99.   Change in angle of insertion of deep flexor tendon on the coffin bone if navicular bone were absent (top). When navicular bone is present, (bottom) the movement of the coffin joint does not change the angle of insertion of the deep flexor tendon.

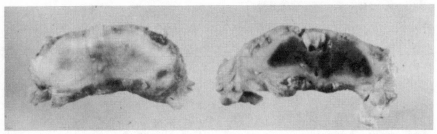

Fig. 100.   Navicular disease. Both bones are damaged, the one on the right being most severe. The dark color indicates destruction of the normally opaque white fibrocartilage on the back surface of the navicular bone.

Navicular disease is an arthrosis developing on the surfaces of the navicular bone and the deep flexor tendon (Fig. 100). The cartilage and tendon are damaged first, followed by changes in the navicular bone itself. Osteophytes then appear. Many people have said and still do say that the first changes are within the bone. On the basis of my autopsy experience, this is simply and clearly not true.

An interesting exception to this statement is the development of osteophytes on the medial and lateral ends of the navicular bone *without* damage to the navicular, deep flexor surfaces. This occurs, most obviously, in horses with contracted tendons or with a very upright pastern (the same difference). Without pursuing the details, these osteophytes appear because of snapping and jerking of the suspensory ligament of the navicular bone. This ligament runs from

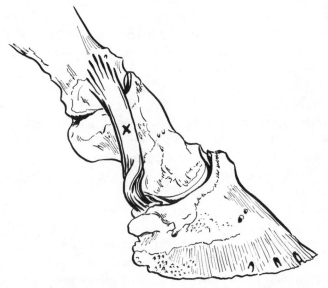

Fig. 101.   The suspensory ligament of the navicular bone (X).

the end of the navicular to attach on the lower end of the long pastern bone, just above the pastern joint (Fig. 101). With the upright pastern conformation there is a tendency for the pastern joint to wobble back and forth, and this wobbling jerks the ligament which jerks on the end of the navicular bone, and new bone formation is the result (Figs. 102, 103). The same remedial measures that we shall recommend for navicular disease also apply in this case (see below).

The arthrosis develops because of vibration and friction between the navicular and the tendon. Vibration occurs for many reasons: too high heels, too low heels; very hard ground; foot too small for the size of the horse either genetically, as with many Quarter Horses, or because of too enthusiastic trimming; pain in the foot: the horse may put his foot on the ground improperly because he knows it is going to hurt. The *pointing* of a horse with navicular disease when standing may well have a dynamic counterpart. That is, he will tend to land toe first, instead of the proper heel first, because there is pain in the heel area. This leads to the same mechanical situation, snapping down of the heel to the ground, as with the low heel conformation. I think you can see how the story develops: a low heel may tend to navicular disease, navicular disease leads to pain, which leads to the horse putting his foot down as if he had an even lower heel.

Hard ground may lead to navicular disease even in a horse with a well-built, well-trimmed hoof. If the hoof is the slightest bit off to begin with, hard ground adds to the equation.

Show jumpers are particularly prone to this disease, as are hunters. It is rare indeed in flat runners or harness horses. As pointed out to me by Dr. Dan Marks, show jumpers describe a steeper parabola over their high jumps than do hunters or steeplechasers, on the average. The show jumper tends to land with his foot as shown in Fig. 104, left, while the hunter lands as in Fig. 104, right. The latter is proper. In the former the digit position is improper, and vibration will occur when the foot hits the ground. Also show jumpers may jump more in a given season, carry heavier riders, and may be heavier themselves than the long-distance hunter: a multiple factor equation as with so many lamenesses of the horse.

I should note that navicular disease is rarely seen in the hind feet, though it does occur.

A fascinating aspect of navicular disease is that it is not nearly as common as most people, including veterinarians, think. It is diagnosed frequently in flat runners, and in some places, at least, in harness horses. In fact, it rarely occurs in these animals. We do have a condi-

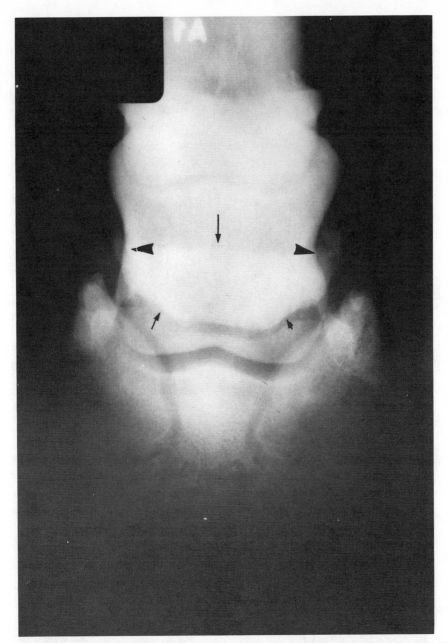

Fig. 102. *Spurs on ends of navicular bone (large arrow heads). The small arrows show the outline of the navicular bone. Such spurs (osteophytes) may occur with navicular-deep flexor damage or in the absence of such damage (contracted tendon, upright pastern). See text for details.*

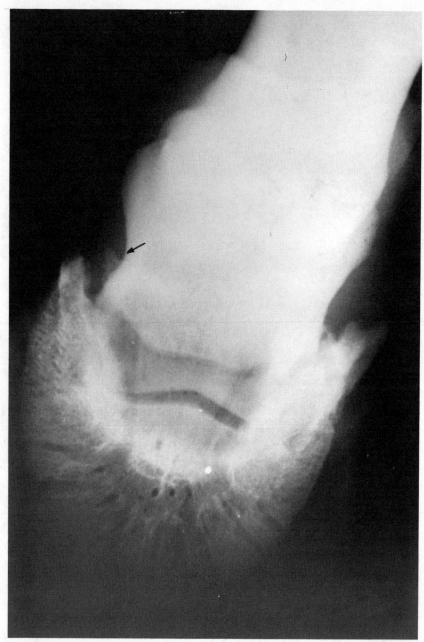

Fig. 103. An oblique view showing a spur on the end of the navicular bone (arrow).

Fig. 104. Show jumper landing (left) and hunter landing (right). The latter is landing normally, that is, more like the normal gallop. The steep angle of landing of the show jumper is related to the development of navicular disease.

tion in those animals which we can call *naviculoid* disease (like navicular disease). This is a soreness in the heel region that responds to hoof testers and blocks out when the nerve (heel nerve) to that area is blocked with anesthetic solution. Being honest, I have no exact idea what the lesion is; but it is clear that it is not damage to the navicular. This navicularlike disease is associated with the low, underrun heel and the long toe. For the time being, at least, I think it might be a tearing and bruising of the laminae that attach the heel and quarter of the hoof to the underlying tissues. When the heel is kept too short there is less tissue to absorb the shock of landing, and vibration can occur, damaging the sensitive laminae. Also, the insta- bility and necessity to lift the body weight because of the hoof not cutting into the ground can add further complications.

TRIMMING THE HOOF

Since I have said so much about this long-toe, low-heel situation, perhaps it would be worthwhile to digress and consider why so many horses are trimmed that way. First of all, and this is true, the wall is thinner at the quarters and heels. The hurried, careless blacksmith can rasp them away much more quickly than he can the thicker wall at the toe. Second, racehorse trainers feel that a horse can go faster, sprint faster, with this type of foot. That may be true. The horse can accelerate himself faster as the foot is leaving the ground. That is because with the longer toe there is a greater moment arm. That means the horse can exert more force against the ground by contracting his deep flexor muscle. The mass is the same. Therefore, since force equals mass multiplied by acceleration, and we increase the force, we increase the acceleration. Ergo, the horse goes faster. Note, however, that the horse has to increase the force developed by the deep flexor muscle, which means it is working harder which means it will tire, fatigue, earlier. When that muscle becomes fatigued, it cannot position the hoof properly for impact with the ground. In fact it will land heavily on the heel with the toe up. This is the same as the high heel (too high heel) conformation, which leads to vibration and damage either to the navicular or the laminae.

How do we prevent navicular disease? Let the horse wear his foot naturally barefoot, and then trim him the way he wears. The horse wears his foot the way he does because that is what is mechanically and biologically correct for him. Your eye and ideas are not nearly as good as nature's.

How do you keep him going when he does have navicular disease? Shorten the toe and raise the heel, making it easier for him to break over, thereby reducing the force the deep flexor muscle has to exert and thereby easing the pain. Cutting of the heel nerves is undoubtedly resorted to too often. It is not a cure but, rather, a last-ditch, desperation measure. All too often, complete return to soundness does not result and, eventually, the damage to the deep flexor tendon will become so extensive that the tendon will rupture, and that is the end of the horse. In my opinion, and that of many veterinarians whose opinion I respect, heel nerving should never be done. If shoeing and proper trimming do not provide at least working soundness, the horse should be retired.

Navicular bones do fracture occasionally (Fig. 105). Most of the time they break as the result of damage to the bone with long-standing navicular disease. Rarely one may break as a single event fracture. This is simply an exaggeration of the several types of misstep we have discussed as the cause of navicular disease. Such fractures seem to be more common in Quarter Horses, particularly the big plow horse body types with the spindly legs and small feet. One may help a horse with a fractured navicular bone with a full-bar shoe plus a long rest period (one year). Nerving is effective in negating the pain, but generally such horses will not last long as useful animals.

I might also note at this point that navicular bones can be subject to congenital malformation. I have seen one case (thanks to Dr.

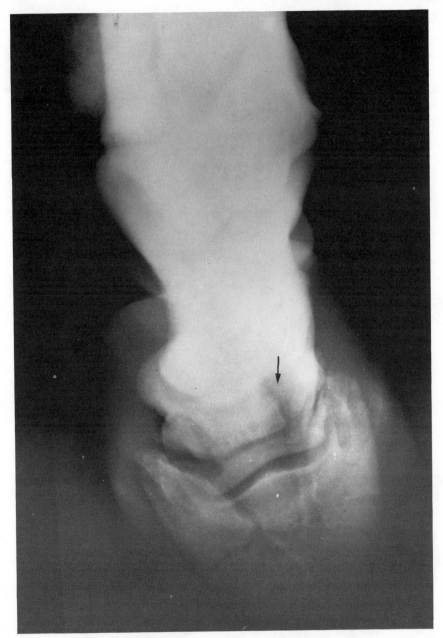

Fig. 105. Fracture of the navicular bone (arrow).

Charles Reid of New Bolton Center, Kennett Square, Pennsylvania)
that had no navicular bone. There have been a few others in which the
bone formed from several different ossification centers instead of one,

giving the bone a lobated appearance (Fig. 106). There have, however, not been enough of these cases followed long enough to allow
us to say whether this predisposes the animal to navicular disease or
fracture. The important point, for now, is that you may see lines like
those in Fig. 106 on radiographs of the navicular bone of young horses
before they have been broken. They are not necessarily fractures!

LAMINITIS

The horse is almost unique in his affliction with this terrible
condition. There are several types of laminitis. The first is classical
founder. It often involves the newly foaled mare who has not passed

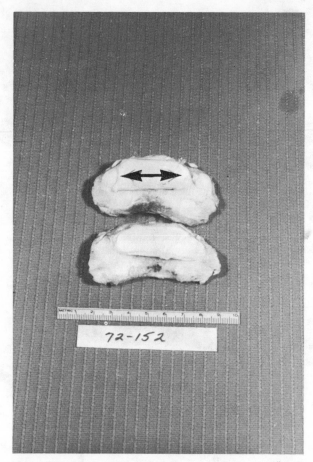

*Fig. 106. Navicular bone that formed from three ossification centers: a
central and one at each end. Arrows point to lines indicating demarcation of
the two ends from the middle part.*

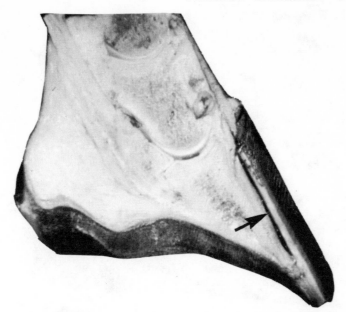

Fig. 107. Acute laminitis. The sensitive and insensitive laminae have been destroyed and replaced by a pool of dark blood. Arrow points to this area between the coffin bone and the hoof wall.

her afterbirth or the horse of any type that has overeaten or overdrunk. The feet are hot, extremely painful, and the animal may be unwilling to move. Keeping it simple, this is a severe destruction of the sensitive laminae of the hoof (Fig. 107). With good luck the damage repairs, and the animal goes on. With severe damage the coffin bone rotates down because the laminae, which hold it in place, have been destroyed (Fig. 108). The mechanism by which this destruction occurs is not known. With the knowledge we have today the answer could probably be forthcoming. In any event, it appears that some toxic product is formed, usually in the intestine, which travels through the bloodstream and damages the laminae, and/or the blood vessels to the laminae, resulting in death of the tissue.

The second type of laminitis occurs in one foot when the horse, because of severe lameness, fracture or radial paralysis, for example, is unable to use the other foreleg to support weight. This is more likely to occur if the three-legged animal is confined to a stall. If the animal is turned out, it will move around somewhat by hopping and using the hind legs well under the body. Such motion, no matter how small will help to pump venous blood back up the leg. This will prevent stasis of blood in the hoof and the subsequent decreased

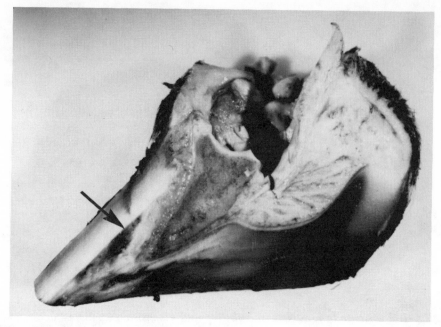

Fig. 108. Chronic laminitis. The coffin bone has rotated away from the hoof wall. Arrow indicates area of wide separation of coffin bone from hoof wall.

oxygen supply which leads to necrosis (death) of the laminae. As I am sure you know, there is virtually no muscle in the lower part of the horse's limb, and the return of blood from the limb is in large part accomplished by the pumping action of the hoof. When that pumping action is lost, the venous return is impaired.

The third type may be called road founder or pony founder, and it is very common. The fat pony is put on lush pasture in the spring of the year and founders. During the late fall and winter, the pony generally loses some weight, and the signs of laminitis may subside, only to reappear in the spring with the new grass. This is not the same type of laminitis that we have been describing above, at least as far as we know at present. It is, rather, a tearing of the laminae at the toe because the toe is too long, and the pony is too fat (Fig. 109). There is greater resistance to elevation of the pastern because of increased body weight and because of the long toe. This is particularly obvious in Shetland ponies. Perhaps the reason is that Shetlands were selected for the Shetland Islands. The Shetland Island soil is stony and rough, and pasturage is not abundant. The ponies were adapted to this environment. Taken from this habitat which they fit so well,

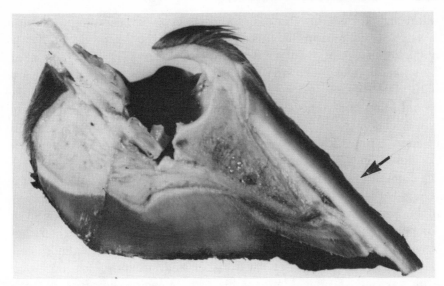

Fig. 109. Pony-type laminitis. The coffin bone is torn away from the wall close to the toe (arrow). Note the length of the toe in this case as compared to the more normal toe in Fig. 107.

with ground to wear away their iron-hard little hooves and limited pasturage, they now reside in lush pastures on relatively soft ground and get very little work. It is also obvious that most people neglect trimming a pony's feet.

I am not implying that ponies never get classical laminitis, or that horses never get the pony, toe-tearing type; they do. It is simply that one type is more common in certain animals than others. For example, so-called road founder may be of this toe-tearing type: the big, tired horse, worked all day on hard going, such as roads. I believe it is true that heavy carriage horses of an earlier day were often afflicted with this road founder condition.

So, once again, the question: What do we do about it? And once again I think the answer insofar as prevention is concerned is quite obvious. In this, as so many other things regarding lameness in horses, there is one essential point to remember, and it is the one most frequently forgotten. Indeed I think many horsemen and veterinarians have never thought of it. We are so extraordinarily selfish, we humans, that we think everything in nature is there for our benefit and use and, that it must, necessarily, adapt itself to that purpose. Unfortunately for everybody that is not true. Coal, oil, etc. were not put in the ground for man's use. They occurred by natural processes, and man has taken them for his use. In so doing he pollutes. The horse was not designed by nature for man's use. He evolved according to natural laws as an animal unto himself. Man took the horse, as he has so many other things, and put him to man's use. We must remember, however, that we are using the horse for purposes other than those natural and proper to the horse himself. No horse in his right mind would jump over fences chasing some hapless fox, any more than he would choose to pull a brewery wagon or participate in that insanity of former times known as a cavalry charge. When we ask horses to do these things, then, we must reap the consequences.

Laminitis is a clear example of what I have been saying. In nature horses eat forage: grass, green or dry. They do not eat large quantities of high-protein grain rations or rich alfalfa hay. Alfalfa hay is great for perverting cattle, making them grow faster and fatter than they should. Is that what is wanted for a horse? Horses eat almost continuously in the wild. They eat a rather small quantity at a time over a long period of time. Man, for his own purposes, however, requires a horse to eat most of his daily supply of food at two or three sittings and often keeps him locked up in a stall in between. Husbandry conditions such as this obviously set up the basic conditions for the development of classical-type laminitis. I can remember working draft horses to the plow or cultivator from seven in the morning until noon, without allowing them a drop of water. We *were* smart enough to allow them only a little water at a time, so they would not founder. I stopped at the end of every row for a drink when cultivating corn in midsummer; the poor horse, with a greater need, had to wait four or five hours.

The prevention of pony-type laminitis is certainly obvious. Trim your Shetland's hooves, restrict his diet to something like that of his natural environment, and this form of founder should virtually disappear.

Suppose laminitis, classical type, does occur. What to do? Call for veterinary help immediately. Stand the horse in cool water, and pull his shoes. The veterinarian will radiograph the involved feet to determine the degree of coffin bone rotation and act accordingly.

SIDEBONE

There are fibrocartilages within the horse's foot, attached on either side to the coffin bone, extending backward inside the quarters. We have already discussed their function. Normally these cartilages ossify (convert to bone) slowly with age. If they ossify earlier or more rapidly than normal, it is called sidebone and can sometimes be asso-

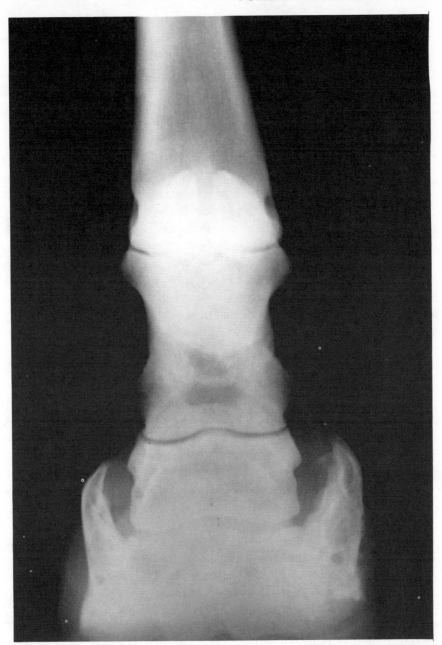

Fig. 110. Sidebone involving both lateral cartilages.

ciated with a significant amount of lameness (Fig. 110). The cause of this premature ossification is not completely clear. However, it is, in general, seen more often in heavier animals on hard working surfaces, and is a slow-speed concussion lesion.

The base-wide (that is, the feet placed out wider than the body) and/or toed-out conformation tends to cause inside (medial) sidebone while the base narrow (feet placed close together under the body) tends to cause outside (lateral) sidebone. J. A. W. Dollar made the interesting observation that sidebone, occurring in heavy horses working on hard ground, most frequently involved the lateral cartilage of the left foreleg. This localization may be explained as follows. The heavy draft teams of earlier times were, as a rule, trained to turn to the left (near) rather than the right (off) side. Under draft, turning to the left, the horse would tend to place the left foreleg under the body, resulting in a functional base-narrow conformation.

As indicated above the cause of side-bone is not exactly understood, and it is not always easy to determine whether the presence of this ossification is associated with lameness. One can find the ossified cartilages on the radiographs with or without signs of lameness. As a rule of thumb sidebone is less of a problem in the open, well-made foot and becomes more of a problem when the hoof is small and/or contracted. The only effective treatment is to trim and handle the hoof in the way in which one would counteract contracted heels.

CONTRACTED HOOF

As we have already discussed, part of the energy (concussion) absorption mechanism of the foot is the expansion of the quarters and compression of the digital cushion. If these two mechanisms are not operating, or not operating adequately, one expects to see a sore, tender-foot horse. The loss of these two mechanisms is most commonly the result of contracted hooves. This condition is characterized by a narrowing or pinching-in of the heels with narrowing of the frog and the clefts (Fig. 111). The general appearance, from the rear view, is that of a human foot in spiked heels. The cause or causes of this condition are not completely clear in many cases. There is no real relationship to the overall size of the foot. The pony or mule has a small foot, but it is not necessarily contracted. The most common cause is undoubtedly improper shoeing and trimming. Some blacksmiths seem to have a traditional dislike for the bars and will, on the slightest provocation, cut them out before doing anything else. The bar is there for a reason and that reason is, primarily, to prevent the quarters and heels from moving in too far. With the bars present the springlike hoof wall cannot move in or out too far. With the bars absent it can do both and, because the hoof is very much like a spring, it will tend, in the long run, to move in, contract.

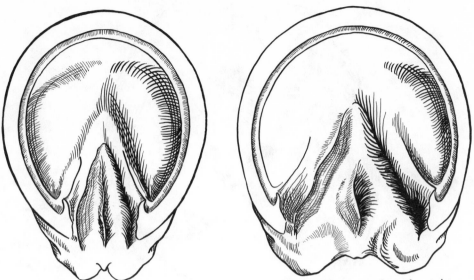

Fig. 111. Contracted foot on the left as compared to the normal on the right.

With contraction of the foot, the quarters and heels cannot move normally and the outward expansion of the compressed digital cushion is inhibited. With the loss of these two shock-absorption devices the shock will be felt in other parts of the foot, and the horse may be lame.

CORN

Horses with contracted feet are also subject to the condition known as corn. This is a bruising of the sole in the area of the angle of the bar. Leaving shoes on the hooves too long is one of the more common causes of corns. Race horses are generally reset and replated regularly, but turn-outs, saddle horses, and backyard horses may not be replated frequently enough. Even with racehorses the careless or overworked shoer may "make do" with an improperly fitted shoe, setting the foot up for corn. The properly fitted shoe will appear as in Fig. 112. The heel of the shoe will be set out slightly wider than the hoof at the quarter. As the heel of the foot expands upon impact with the ground, the hoof wall slides out on the shoe. As the hoof grows, it pulls the initially properly fitting shoe forward, toward the toe, as shown in Fig. 113. It is obvious that, as the foot impacts, the heel of the shoe will be driven upward against the angle of the wall and bar: bruising = corn. Similarly, if the shoe is too small or fabricated so that the heel of the shoe is in position over the angle, a corn is almost inevitable.

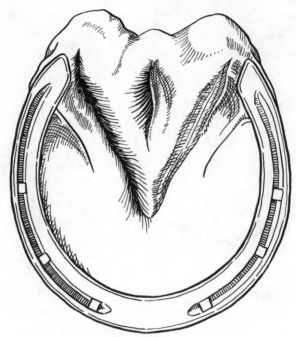

Fig. 112. Properly fitted horseshoe.

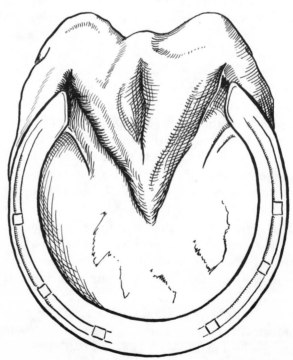

Fig. 113. Improperly fitted horseshoe or one which has been left on too long. Heels of shoe now press on the angle of the bar and the wall and can cause corn.

I doubt very much that we need to discuss prevention or cure of either contracted hoof or corn. Surely that is obvious once their causes are understood!

HOOF CRACKS

Cracks in the wall of the hoof may be classified in a number of ways. If on the sides of the hoof, they are known as quarter cracks and, if toward the front of the hoof, as toe cracks (Figs. 114, 115).

The crack may begin at the coronet or at the bearing edge of the hoof wall. The latter are the more common and particularly so at the quarters. Of course, if not properly cared for such a crack at the lower edge of the wall can extend all the way up to the coronet.

First, let us consider some of the causes of quarter cracks. One of the essential requirements of the hoof wall is that it be elastic, able to bend and regain its original shape again as the load is applied and

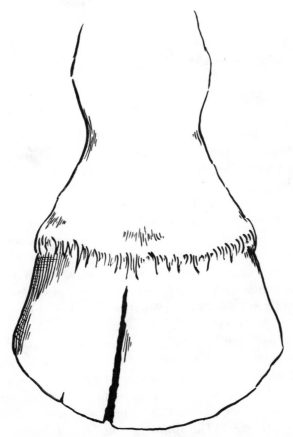

Fig. 114. A toe crack.

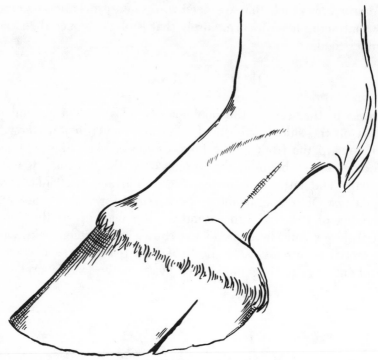

Fig. 115. A quarter crack.

then taken off the hoof. If this essential elasticity is lost, the hoof wall will tend to crack or split. Such splits will naturally tend to follow the preexisting anatomical structure—the vertically oriented horn tubules.

The elasticity of the hoof wall is dependent upon a number of factors only a few of which are understood in any detail at the present time. One important and fairly well understood factor, however, is moisture. The hoof wall must be moist in order to be properly elastic.

We may use a natural sponge as an analogy. When moist, saturated with water, the sponge readily bends or compresses when squeezed and pops quickly back to its original shape when released. If allowed to dry out, on the other hand, the sponge will break or crumble when force is applied. Another analogy is the age-old carpenter's or ship-wright's technique for bending beams of wood into curved shapes. The beam is subjected to steam (water vapor) until thoroughly soaked. It is then bent and held in the bent position with clamps. When the beam has dried thoroughly, the clamps are removed, and it stays in the curved position. The shipwright makes the beam elastic—bendable—by soaking it with water. When the beam loses the water, it loses its elasticity, and stays in the bent position.

As is well-recognized, then, the hoof must be elastic, and it must be moist in order to be elastic. How do we keep the hoof moist? Well, we should do it in the most natural possible way—the way nature intended. In the normal hoof there is a thick layer of vertical horn tubules, which provide the strength and elasticity of the hoof wall. There is, in addition, a thin layer of very dense, shiny plates of horn which covers the outside of this thick, tubular layer. This outer layer is called the *periople*. It grows downward continuously from the coronary band along with the horn tubules. Its major function is undoubtedly to provide a seal in order to keep moisture in the horn tubule layer.

Many of you may, by now, have recognized a very serious flaw in the work of the average or poor horseshoer. Having trimmed the hoof, nailed, and clinched the shoe, the broad rasp goes on, removing all the shiny perioplic layer. The wall is left somewhat grayish and fuzzy. In order to smooth and "neat up" the job, the shoer now paints the wall with some form of hoof dressing, which makes the wall dark and shiny. The beauty, however, is only skin deep. The protective periople has been removed, the hoof dressing is no replacement, and water will be surely and steadily lost from the horn tubules. Elasticity will inevitably decrease and wall cracks eventually occur.

Why has this habit of rasping away the periople developed? Simply, I think, because it is rough, often uneven and, when left alone, the hoof does not appear as neat and orderly as man thinks it should be. But, leave it alone! Better a somewhat less than machine-made look than a crack.

Cracks are more common in the quarter than in the toe; why? The normal action of the hoof wall is to absorb impact when the hoof strikes the ground. To do so the horny wall both compresses and bends. Since the wall at the quarter is thinner than the wall at the toe, the quarter will bend and move more than the toe.

The movement of the quarters, as everyone knows, is outward; that is, the heels expand, spread, as the hoof contacts the ground and the weight of the horse is applied to the hoof. This outward expansion serves two purposes: absorbing impact energy and allowing the digital cushion to expand as the bones of the pastern move down and press upon it. This expansion of the digital cushion also absorbs impact energy. The digital cushion is a firm, spongy mass of fat and elastic tissue that forms the bulbs of the heel, filling the space between frog and quarters.

One could quickly jump on the obvious bandwagon and say: well, of course, if the quarters move more they are naturally more subject to cracking and breaking. Since the quarters are normally constructed to move, however, this explanation is too superficial indeed. There are, in fact, a number of reasons why quarter cracks occur. First, if the periople is removed as already described, the wall of the hoof tends to dry out. Once dried out, the greater movement of the quarter then predisposes it to cracking.

A second and important factor is the process of shoeing. The shoe is nailed to the toe and quarters but not to the heels. When force is applied, then, the heels move out while the quarters and toe are restricted in their movement, fastened by the nails to the shoe. This creates an abnormal bending force a short distance behind (toward the heel, in the quarter) the last nail.

This unhappy state of affairs cannot be rectified by more nails placed in the heel. The wall is too thin to hold the nail, the attempt to move is still there, and cracks will occur with the nail hole as the weak point.

Hoof trimming, if improperly done, can lead to quarter cracks. If the bars are cut away and the heels allowed to contract, the wall at the quarters can become too vertical rather than sloping outward. Abnormal forces are now applied to the wall and cracking may occur.

If the web of the shoe is set in, so that the bearing edge of the wall at the quarter overhangs, excessive force will be applied to the wall where the overhang begins—you guessed it—quarter crack.

If one examines the hoof wall of a horse allowed to run barefooted for some time, it is apparent that the ground surface of the wall is not a straight line. It is slightly concave beginning at about the middle of the side wall back through the quarter. The reasons for this have not been clearly worked out, but it is definitely normal for a barefoot horse and is probably a function of the hoof cutting into the ground. If a shoe is now placed on this foot, the force is concentrated at each end of the concavity, and a crack can appear near the middle of the concavity.

Then there is the horse born with a dry, shelly hoof who gets quarter cracks no matter what one does. Everyone knows what a shelly hoof looks like, but does anyone know what it really is? Though such horses, and such hooves, have been with us for a long time, I am not aware of any serious attempt to find out precisely what is wrong. It might be suggested that there is a defect in the normal growth and development of the horn much in the way some women have nails that continually split. That is, the shelly hoof is one that does not have an adequate outer covering to prevent loss of water from the horn tubules. Such a defective periople can be man-made as we have already discussed or it may be congenital, nutritional, or whatever.

Cracks in the wall of the hoof are a serious nuisance. Many of them are preventable by careful shoeing, trimming, etc. The predisposition to cracks, apart from the shelly hoof, must be attributed to the fact that we shoe horses. In this area two major scientific investigations are needed: how to shoe horses better and discovering the cause of shelly feet.

I shall not enter upon a discussion of how to handle the crack once it has appeared. That is a matter which is best left to your veterinarian and horseshoer, hopefully working in concert.

OTHER FOOT DISORDERS

We have by no means exhausted the possibilities for something to go wrong with the foot. Let us quickly run through a few more of them. Nail pricks are really quite obvious. The only problem may be that the smith does not know or chooses to hide the fact that he got too close with the nail. If the horse walks away from the smith sore, look for that close nail, and the spot of blood (though the hoof dressing painted over the destroyed periople may hide it).

It is not rare for a horse to pick up a nail or piece of wire in the sole with resulting bleeding, abscessation, and lameness. Careful examination of the bottom of the foot should be the first thing with every new lameness. It has happened to everyone, but I shall tell the story again. As a student we had a horse presented to the school clinic, lame. We students and the intern in charge examined the horse thoroughly, we thought. We had everything diagnosed from popped knee to bicipital bursitis. The owner came in the next day and pulled a nail out of the sole.

Thrush is a nasty, odoriferous disintegration of the frog, clefts, and sometimes the sole itself. While the exact agent or agents causing the problem is/are not known, it is clear that filthy conditions, failure to keep the foot clean, and not allowing proper foot expansion are major factors. Treatment can be long, difficult, and tedious. In essence it consists of careful, frequent trimming and cleaning with application of drying, antiseptic agents.

Canker is a poorly understood malfunctioning of the sensitive, horn-producing membrane usually beginning in or around the frog. Instead of normal horn, a moist, fetid exudate is produced together with abnormal horn. It was, apparently, somewhat more common in the draft breeds. Treatment consists of continuous, careful removal of diseased tissue and the application of astringent antiseptics. Exercise should continue because, for some unknown reason, it appears to be beneficial; perhaps it allows the foot to expand and "breathe."

Keratoma is an uncommon, benign tumor of the wall horn that can cause pressure and pain. Once the pain is located by percussion (tapping that is), hoof testers and radiographs the only treatment is surgical removal.

Seedy toe is a separation of the wall from the sole at the toe. Its cause is often the result of chronic laminitis or the road founder already discussed. Proper trimming, avoiding the long toe, is the obvious solution.

Gravel is an infection that gains entrance through the bottom of the hoof, particularly near or at the junction of the wall and sole. Generally such horses are acutely lame. The infection may work its way upward until it breaks out at the coronary band. This is quite reasonable since the normal pumping action of the foot (the mechanism for the return of venous blood up the leg) will push the infection upward as well. This is a matter for immediate veterinary attention.

FRACTURE—COFFIN BONE

The coffin bone may be likened to a glass marble dropped on a sheet of foam rubber (the laminae and digital cushion). Upon impact, the foam rubber yields under the force of the falling marble. It then rebounds, throwing the marble (coffin bone) up again. If the same marble were dropped upon concrete (from a sufficient height), it would shatter upon impact because concrete is not nearly so elastic as foam rubber.

If the elastic structures of the foot (laminae or cushion) are not working properly (not sufficiently elastic), fracture may occur (Figs. 116, 117). Conversely, if the ground upon which the hoof lands is very hard, and the force of the horse's weight sufficiently great, the total impact may exceed the normal elastic potential of the laminae and cushion.

The foot may be improperly positioned when it strikes the ground so that the impact is borne by one part of the hoof and coffin bone more than another, overwhelming the elastic potential of that one part.

An important type of coffin bone fracture may follow infection (pus gaining entrance to the inside of the hoof). Such infections typically infiltrate and dissect through the tissues and may destroy

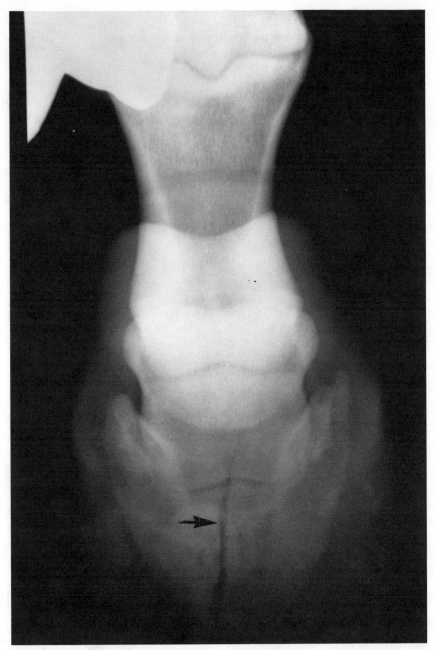

Fig. 116.   Fracture of the coffin bone.

parts of the laminae and the cushion, thus reducing the elasticity. The infection may also invade the coffin bone itself, destroying bone tissue, weakening it and permitting the normal impact forces to cause fracture.

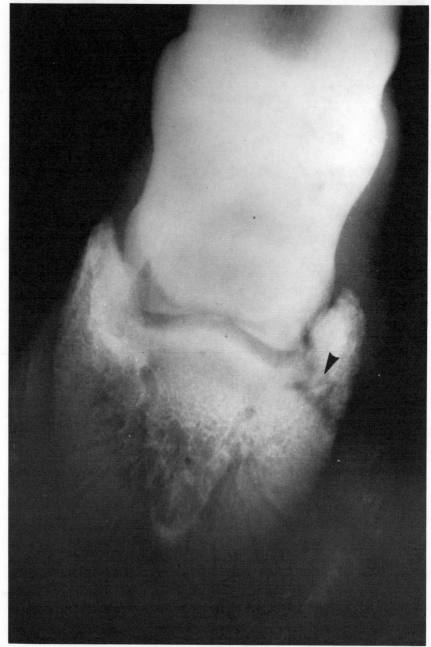

Fig. 117. Fracture of the wing of the coffin bone.

There are no satisfactory statistics to indicate the frequency of occurrence of coffin bone fracture (or any other lameness, for that matter). I can say only that they are not so common as sesamoid fractures nor so rare as navicular disease in racehorses.

Greatly oversimplified, salient factors in fractures of the coffin bone may be summarized as follows:

Force too great—fracture

Bone weak or weakened (as by infection or nerving)—fracture.

Springs (laminae and cushions) weak or weakened—fracture

Surface too hard—fracture

Force applied unevenly (improper hoof placement)—fracture

Which of these factors or combinations of factors may be operating in any given case is often difficult to decide. As a rule of thumb, usually at least two factors will be operating simultaneously.

TENDON INJURIES

I have saved this topic for a separate section because injuries of this sort are one of the most important and disastrous problems that can happen to the working horse. We have several major categories to consider: bowed tendon, check ligament strain, and pulled suspensory. We shall also discuss briefly another previously undescribed type of suspensory damage.

Bowed Tendon

Bowed tendon is one of the most common cripplers of horses (Fig. 118). There has been much controversy over the years about the precise nature of this condition. It is readily recognized as a clinical entity, but, until recent years, has not been well described pathologically. It is now abundantly clear that the common bow is the result of tearing of the connective tissue fibers that comprise the superficial flexor tendon. The greatest majority of such tears occur in the middle third of the tendon (Figs. 119, 120). Occasionally a horse comes out of a workout or race with obvious pain, evident by the gait and on pressure over the tendon. In a few hours there is obvious heat and swelling, the *bow*. More often than not, however, the careful horseman may detect something considerably less obvious than this some time before the full-blown bow appears. The horse comes out of his workout very slightly lame, if at all. Careful palpation along the course of the superficial flexor may reveal a slightly tender area with a slight increase in temperature. This is slight tearing of the tendon, the first beginnings of a bow. Unhappily, the human response to this early change is usually ice, paint, antiphlogistine, mud, or some such, and back to work the next day or the day after. Often the horseman calls this stage a *rap*, thinking the animal interfered. Maybe, but do not believe

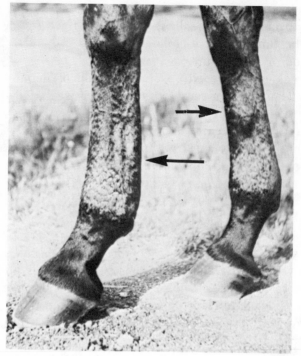

Fig. 118. Bowed tendon (lower arrow) of left foreleg. There is also a splint (upper arrow) on the right foreleg.

it! Treat as a bow until proven otherwise.

If you cut yourself, how long does it take to heal? Seven days to maybe ten or twelve days, depending upon you and how old you are. How long will it take that slight tear of the horse's tendon to heal: about the same time or longer. The repair tissue, the scar, will be disorganized connective tissue fibers. The collagen or connective tissue fibers of the tendon are precisely oriented and lined up parallel to the long axis of the tendon. This is for a good reason. The tensile strain on the tendon is parallel to the long axis and so the fibers must be lined up the same way. When the scar tissue, a feltwork of collagen fibers, forms, however, it does not form in this nicely lined-up manner. When the tendon moves, those young fibers not lined up properly will be retorn; thus, new swelling and soreness. Eventually, the tearing of the misaligned fibers will stop because most or all of the fibers are lined up properly. The bow is now healed. This can take a month to a year depending upon how many fibers were torn to start with. A moderate amount of tensile strain, pulling on the tendon, during healing is a good thing. The strain field set up will tend to guide the

Fig. 119. Comparison of bowed tendon (the thickened, enlarged tendon to the left) with the opposite normal tendon from the same horse (right).

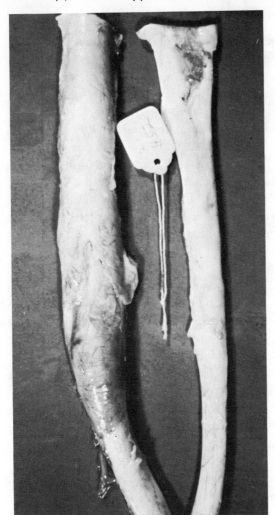

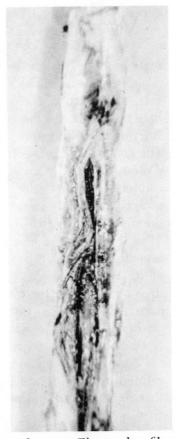

Fig. 120. An acute bowed tendon seen from the rear. The tendon fibers are torn, disorganized, and there is bleeding (dark areas).

newly forming collagen fibers into the proper orientation. Too much work, however, will tear them before they can line up properly.

The first, apparently minor, signs of pain over the superficial flexor tendon must, then, be taken very seriously. A month is not too long to rest or at least severely limit the exercise of that horse. There are a number of things you can do during that rest period which we shall talk about as we go along.

Getting into some detail, the superficial flexor tendon almost always tears somewhere near its middle, at least in its middle third, and the tear invariably begins on the back surface. This is not hard to figure out. If you take a cable or string, rubber band, or some such, and pull it apart until it breaks, it will break near the middle. If you pull that rubber band around a pulley and pull until it begins to break (not an easy trick to accomplish, you usually go too far), it will begin to fail or break near the middle and on the surface farthest from the pully. In other words, the tendon will fail on the back surface first because that surface is under greatest tension because that surface is farthest from the center of rotation at the fetlock joint.

As the tendon tears, there is edema, hemorrhage, swelling, etc. Whether that is small scale or large scale, the only recourse is to wait for healing to occur and for a full-blown bow that is one year minimum.

Why does it tear? The subject is complicated. First, the tendon tears because it is put under excessive tension. This excessive tension is applied to the tendon during the second half of the stride (from the vertical position of the cannon, when the fetlock is fully down, to the time the foot leaves the ground). The problem occurs while the pastern is trying to elevate, move up again. What happens is shown in Fig. 121. The downward force being exerted on the leg is too great to allow the pastern to lift. The forward momentum of the horse's body, however, continues and the fetlock overdorsiflexes. This puts more strain on the superficial flexor tendon than on the deep flexor or suspensory, because the superficial is farther from the point of rotation of the fetlock joint. Also, at this time, the superficial flexor muscle attached to the tendon is contracting. At a time when the tendon should be shortening because of its own innate elasticity and the pull of the muscle, it is being stretched because the pastern cannot elevate and the fetlock is over-dorsiflexing. Result: tearing of the tendon.

Let us list the reasons for this delay in pastern elevation:

1. Overweight: too much downward force on too little horse.

2. A normal amount of weight improperly applied. The forces exerted on the leg are basically of three types, and it is important that those three be in proper relationship to each other. Simply put,

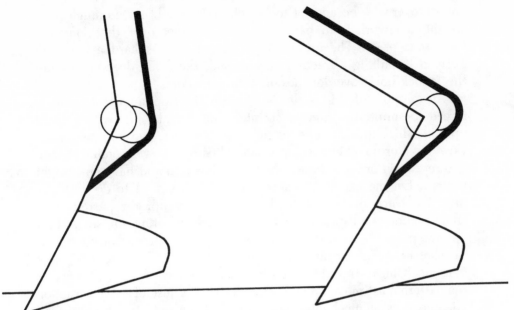

Fig. 121. The immediate cause of bowed tendon. On the left the pastern has elevated normally during the second half of the support phase of the stride. The superficial flexor tendon is represented by the heavy, black line. On the right, the pastern has not elevated sufficiently, but the horse has continued forward, overflexing the fetlock and causing great strain of the superficial flexor tendon.

if the horse places his front leg too far underneath his body, such as leaning into a very sharp turn, the three forces get out of balance, the downward force becomes too great, and we have the same effect as the simple overload described in 1.

3. Another type of overload is jumping. When the horse has to come down from a high jump, the load will be much greater than if running along on the flat.

4. Slipping. When the hoof slips backward along the ground, the fetlock rotates, stretching the tendon, but the coffin joint cannot rotate. If the horse does not split his pastern, he may bow.

5. Deep going can also predispose to tearing. The foot sinks so far into the ground that the horse cannot pull it out quickly enough, ergo as in 4.

6. Long-toe, low-heel, delay in breaking the foot over, leads to overdorsiflexion of the fetlock and possible bow. This effect, as all the others noted above, will be enhanced by fatigue. The flexor muscles tire from too much work, too much work for the condition of the

animal, overwork because of too much body weight or too much rider weight, overwork from having to pull the foot over that long toe for a mile or so. The muscles tire, cannot pull as hard and/or are delayed in pulling a fraction of a second; the coffin does not rotate; the fetlock does; overdorsiflexion = torn tendon.

An example of this is the horse with the sloping pastern that is forced to sprint. In order to sprint he must make his pastern more upright which quickly fatigues the flexor muscles, and he must either slow down or possibly develop sesamoiditis or a bowed tendon. I said, and repeat, in order to be a sprinter the horse should have an upright pastern. Let me explain because I feel this has a lot to do with the high incidence of bowed tendons. The short upright pastern is a conformation predisposing to bow. We are selecting for such short upright pasterns because we are selecting for extreme speed in our race horses. Again, we must skip many of the details because it becomes very mechanical. In order to go faster, which means accelerate faster, the pastern must move up and down faster. Because of its construction and the laws of mechanics, however, this can only be accomplished by elevating the pastern. The velocity of movement of the pastern is:

$$u = \frac{\theta}{t}$$

That is, the angular movement (θ) divided by the time (t) available equals the velocity (u). Acceleration is:

$$a = \frac{u}{t}$$

That is, acceleration (a) is equal to the velocity (u) divided by the time (t). In order to increase acceleration we must increase velocity, and since time is limiting because of the structure of the ligaments and tendons, we can only increase velocity significantly by increasing the angular distance (θ). Therefore, we must elevate the pastern in order to increase its acceleration. By an even more complex line of reasoning, which I must omit, the angular acceleration can be further increased by shortening the pastern, decreasing its moment of inertia.

In any case we are selecting horses for extreme speed; by so doing we inadvertently select for shorter, more upright pasterns because horses with extreme speed tend to have that kind of pastern. That is not the only thing that makes a fast horse, obviously, but it is an important factor.

It should be clear what one does to treat bowed tendons once they have occurred. Simply rest, mild and very gradual increasing exercise, trim the foot to normal, shorten the toe and lengthen the heel. Reduce the food intake, particularly the grain. Paints, blisters, firing, etc. will not speed up healing or the orientation of the collagen fibers. Do not cut down the heels with the idea of moving the pastern up and taking the load off the tendon! It will then heal in the shortened position and be even more predisposed to tearing when you start again.

Surgical splitting of the tendon has had a great deal of publicity and favorable reviews in the past few years. The idea is to increase the blood supply to the tendons thereby speeding up healing. I thought this sounded good, but the facts are that only the split part acquires more blood vessels, and there is no evidence that this helps in any way. This whole idea has been rationalized on the basis, scientific on the face of it, that the center of the tendon has a poorer blood supply than the outside. This is not true, but is based on artefacts (made by art) of the injection method used to demonstrate the blood vessels. The outside and inside of the tendon are equally well supplied by vessels as microscopic sections readily show. Also this idea assumes that the tearing occurs first in the center of the tendon and not on the back surface as I have told you. That, too, is not true, and is due to mis-interpretation of the pathology of damaged tendons. The procedure does little harm, perhaps, but no good. Tincture of time and proper handling of feet and horse are the best tendon healers.

PULLED SUSPENSORY LIGAMENT

The powerful suspensory ligament is one of the most fascinating structures in the entire horse economy. Before launching into its problems, let's discuss what it is and what it does.

The suspensory is a thick, heavy band of fibrous tissue that extends from the back of the carpus (knee) to the fetlock. Just above the fetlock it splits into two major branches that attach to the upper part of the sesamoid bones. Two smaller bands run across the fetlock to join the common extensor tendon on the front of the pastern, but they will not concern us now.

A series of short, strong ligaments run from the lower border of the sesamoid bones to attach to the long and short pastern bones. These short ligaments may be thought of as continuous with the suspensory ligament, the sesamoid bones being simply a hard portion of the whole suspensory system or apparatus.

Since the suspensory ligament was, at one time in the phylogenetic history of the horse, a muscle (the interosseous medius muscle), it still contains a quantity of muscle tissue (Fig. 122). The textbooks usually say that this muscle tissue is rudimentary and disappears with age, which is quite untrue. The muscle tissue is abundantly supplied with nerves and serves to damp out, remove vibration when the ligament stretches. Any physical system, such as the suspensory apparatus, tends to vibrate when force is applied to it, and such vibration can be deleterious. A stretched drum head (the suspensory) vibrates when struck with a stick (when the body weight of the horse lands on the leg). The vibration is stopped by placing a hand on the drum head (contraction of the muscle tissue inside the suspensory).

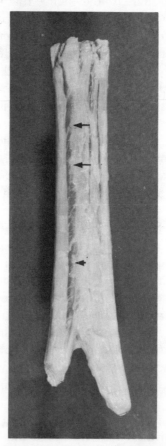

Fig. 122. Suspensory ligament partially dissected. Some of the muscle tissue (grey-brown) is indicated by the arrows.

The suspensory apparatus or system serves to maintain the fetlock in its usual normal position when the horse is standing. If the suspensory is cut above the sesamoids, the fetlock will sink down toward the ground. The two flexor tendons on the back of the leg will prevent complete sinking to the ground. This means that the suspensory serves primarily to prevent rotation of the coffin joint—the joint that rotates to allow the fetlock to move toward the ground.

When the horse is moving, the first structure to take up, receive, the body weight is the suspensory ligament. It yields, stretches, under the force applied by the body weight until about midstride, when the cannon bone is vertical. During the second half of the stride, the stretched ligament shortens, raising the fetlock up again, assisting in propelling the horse forward.

The stretching of the suspensory ligament means that it is absorbing part of the energy imparted by the body weight of the horse. The kinetic energy of the body weight is being converted to potential energy of suspensory ligament displacement until midstride. The ligament obeys (to some extent) the laws of elasticity. It, therefore, reconverts that potential energy gained by downward movement of the fetlock, stretching of the suspensory, back to kinetic energy: shortening of the suspensory and lifting of the fetlock after midstride.

During the course of this down and up movement, undesirable vibration is controlled or dampened by the action of the muscle tissue included within the suspensory ligament. Obviously the suspensory is not the only structure involved, but it is a very important structure.

Although the suspensory divides into two branches above the sesamoids, its overall strength remains the same because the cross sectional area of the two branches equals that of the ligament before branching.

The major type of damage to the suspensory ligament is a partial tearing of one or the other of the two main branches that are attached to the upper part of the proximal sesamoid bones (Fig. 123). Such tearing or *pull* of the suspensory occurs because of uneven or unstable

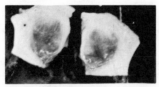

Fig. 123. Cross sections of damaged, torn suspensory ligament branches. The grey-brown discolorations are the damaged areas.

contact of the hoof with the ground. Under this general classification we may include: 1. the hoof itself may be trimmed unevenly; 2. the hoof may impact in the wrong position (tipped to one side or the other); 3. the hoof impacts on uneven ground at high speeds (similar to 2.) The first condition is probably uncommon. The second condition undoubtedly does occur. The foot may not be in the proper position at impact because of fatigue or because the animal was bumped or interfered with, causing the foot to impact improperly. The third condition is probably the most common. Both soft and hard going can lead to suspensory pulls. In soft going, such as damp turf, hooves cut up the ground, and the foot may land on the edge of such a cut-out hole. On hard tracks there may be ridges on the surface for one reason or another (on racetracks these ridges are often the result of heavy tractors, trucks, and harrows). The hoof can land on a ridge and be, therefore, unbalanced. It is clear enough that both cases are essentially the same; greater strain is put on one suspensory branch than on the other and tearing occurs.

The hard surface may also set up another situation leading to torn

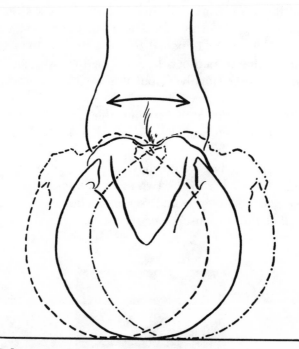

Fig. 124. Schematic of hoof rocking back and forth on the toe when the toe cannot cut into the ground, rear view.

suspensory. The hoof cannot cut into the hard surface. During the second half of the stride, while the leg is propelling, the hoof is forced to break over a narrow contact point at the toe rather than cutting into the ground as we have described previously. This can surely lead to instability, the hoof rocking from side to side with tearing of a suspensory branch the result (Fig. 124).

This is a very serious injury, one which even time has trouble dealing with adequately. There are two reasons for this. One is that the one damaged branch represents almost half the total cross section area of the ligament. Since the strength of any tendon or ligament is, in part, a function of its cross sectional area, the loss of almost half the cross section reduces the strength of the ligament significantly. Secondly, as noted earlier, the suspensory is the main support for the pastern and is constantly under tension when the animal is standing, which makes healing difficult. Unpublished reports, to date, indicate that the tendon-splitting operation may be beneficial in the treatment of pulled suspensory. I frankly do not know what the difference is, if any, between the superficial flexor and the suspensory in this connection. We shall have to await more information. The acute suspensory tear is best handled with a cast—complete immobilization.

There is a second type of suspensory ligament lameness, as yet incompletely defined, but worth describing here. In essence, the lameness is that generally described for *blind splint*. So far as I know blind splint is a myth, but it is considered to be the development of a splint on the inside between the medial splint bone and the cannon bone (and not visible to eye or radiograph). The lameness is said to result from rubbing of the new bone against the side of the suspensory ligament. As noted, I do not believe this entity exists, and the lameness described is what we shall detail below.

Dr. Dan Marks has described the lameness: it occurs in all types of horses. The horse tends to warm out of the lameness, and the lameness is equally severe on soft or hard going. When turned in circles, the horse is lamer when the involved leg is on the outside of the circle (not true of most lamenesses). The animal may move off lamer after pressure is applied to the area between the upper end of the suspensory and the head of the splint bone, just below and in back of the carpus.

I have examined only one such animal at autopsy and found microscopic damage to the small muscle fibers within the suspensory. At the moment I have no idea why this damage occurs and, on the basis of only one case, cannot be sure that is even the real problem. We are still working on it. According to Dr. Marks many horses will recover from this lameness if you simply keep going with them—surprising and gratifying!

Large splints or splint bone fractures can impinge upon the suspensory ligament, causing irritation, fibrosis, and lameness.

PULLED CHECK LIGAMENT

Despite its obvious importance, the deep flexor tendon is rarely damaged except by navicular disease (in fact, navicular disease can become so severe and advanced, particularly after nerving, that the tendon is cut completely in half). The check ligament that runs from the back of the knee to join the deep flexor tendon can, however, be torn (Fig. 125). It appears that the check is damaged more commonly in horses that have to pull a load behind them: draft horses and harness horses. (Jumpers too, may encounter the same problem since, as we shall see below, their knee may buckle forward when landing.) As discussed previously, such animals are predisposed to the knee buckling forward at the time of impact of the forefoot. When the load comes on the leg, immediately after impact, the carpus is snapped into full

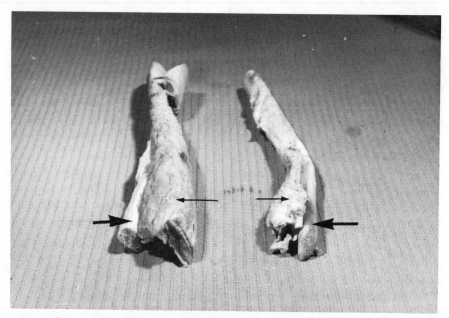

Fig. 125. Strain of deep flexor check ligament. The normal deep flexor (large arrow) and its check ligament (small arrow) are to the right. The damaged check ligament (small arrow) is to the left, together with its deep flexor tendon (large arrow).

extension, straightens out, and the check ligament can be "snapped." This snapping is *abnormal* acceleration, and abnormal acceleration causes damage.

Check ligament strains, like suspensory strains, are very serious and often result in severe limitation of future working usefulness, if not causing permanent retirement. I have no idea how one treats this problem, other than with prolonged rest. Occasionally such horses will return to working soundness. Prevention: don't jump, don't pull loads— don't laugh!

OTHER STRAINS

One of the more common explanations advanced for many vague or poorly understood lamenesses is *sprain, strain,* or tearing of small ligaments around joints or of the joint capsule itself. In fact, most such explanations appear to be fallacious. With the exception of the nonarticular ringbones already described such strains and sprains are extremely rare. It is extraordinarily difficult to tear either the small ligaments or the joint capsule. This diagnosis usually arises when there is obvious pain in the immediate vicinity of a joint, with no changes seen on radiographs. As mentioned previously the radiograph cannot show cartilage damage until it is very far advanced. You had better believe that in such instances the cartilage is damaged and should be treated accordingly.

3

THE NORMAL REARLEG

ALTHOUGH IT MAY COME AS SOMEWHAT OF A SURPRISE, THE REARLEG is very similar to the foreleg. The scapula corresponds to the femur; humerus = tibia; elbow = hock; radius + knee + cannon = rear connon, and the rest is obviously the same. These are not necessarily precise anatomical similarities but, rather, functional similarities (Fig. 126).

I shall start, as with the foreleg, with the foot just clearing the ground and being brought forward, protracting. The hip, stifle, and hock joints all flex, reducing the moment of inertia, enabling the horse to bring the leg forward with the least possible muscular effort, just as with the foreleg. This protraction of the leg and flexion of the several joints is accomplished by a number of muscles working in concert. For simplicity, and referring to Fig. 127, the hip is flexed by the iliopsoas muscle (ilio = haunch, psoas = loin; it is the tenderloin muscle which, in cattle, is called filet mignon). The stifle is flexed by a portion of the biceps femoris (two headed muscle related to the femur). The hock is automatically flexed by an interesting system of muscles on the front and back of the tibia. From the simple model in Fig. 128 you can visualize how this works. Since both the peroneus tertius and superficial flexor are almost entirely tendinous tissue (like the suspensory), the stifle and hock work together, flexing and extending synchronously when the foot is off the ground. Try this on your horse. There is no way you can pick up his foot without the fetlock, hock, and stifle all flexing together. The fetlock must flex, as shown, because of the almost entirely tendinous superficial flexor tendon.

The leg protracts and then begins to swing back in retraction in

160

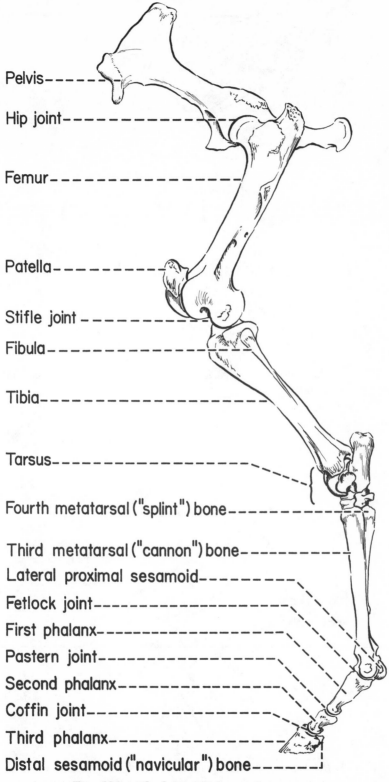

Pelvis

Hip joint

Femur

Patella

Stifle joint

Fibula

Tibia

Tarsus

Fourth metatarsal ("splint") bone

Third metatarsal ("cannon") bone

Lateral proximal sesamoid

Fetlock joint

First phalanx

Pastern joint

Second phalanx

Coffin joint

Third phalanx

Distal sesamoid ("navicular") bone

Fig. 126.   The bones of the rearleg.

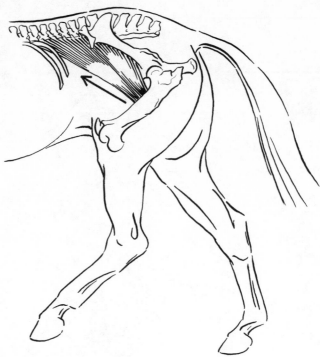

Fig. 127. *Protraction of the rearleg. The iliopsoas muscle (only muscle shown) pulls the leg forward.*

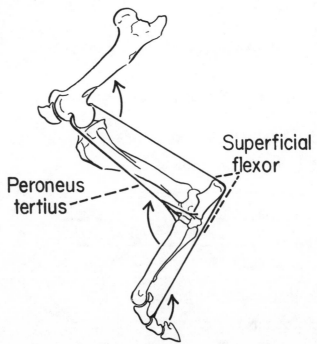

Peroneus
tertius

Superficial
flexor

Fig. 128. *As the leg is protracted, the stifle, hock, and fetlock must all flex together (curved arrows) because the peroneus tertius and the superficial flexor tendons are almost entirely tendinous structures. When one joint flexes, the others must because they are all tied together by these tendinous "straps."*

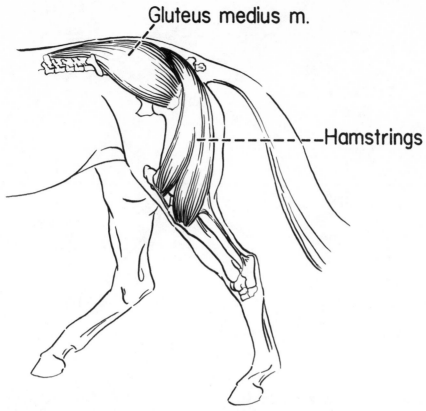

Fig. 129. *Retraction of the rearleg accomplished by the gluteus medius assisted by the hamstring muscles.*

preparation for impact. This retraction is accomplished by several muscles, but I shall consider only a few. The massive gluteus medius (middle muscles of the buttock) is attached as shown in Fig. 129. Its pull rotates the whole leg back. The contraction of the big hamstring muscles assist the gluteus in this backward swing. At the same time the contraction of the quadriceps femoris (four-headed muscle related to the femur) extends the stifle, and of course, this extension of the stifle causes the hock to extend and the fetlock to dorsiflex.

The foot impacts and all these muscles keep right on doing what they were doing before. At the canter and gallop, at least, the location of the center of gravity of the horse's body in front of the rearleg helps to move the rearleg back, assisting the rearleg to carry out its primary function as the major propulsive engine of the horse (Fig. 130). One may note that the human runner can lean forward, so that his center of gravity can assist the legs in the same manner.

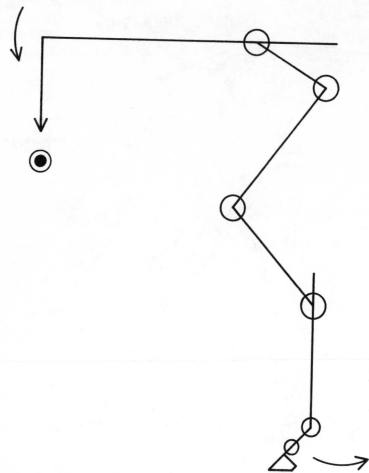

Fig. 130. A schematic drawing of the rearleg, part of the backbone and the center of gravity. When the horse is supported on the rearleg only, the center of gravity, being in front of the leg, tends to rotate the leg back, assisting the leg to move the body forward.

As the rearleg drives back, pushing the horse forward, the hip joint angle opens; the stifle flexes slightly while the hock joint first dorsiflexes and then extends, opening the angle. Remember I said above that, with the foot off the ground, the hock and stifle work together. When propelling the horse, foot on the ground, however, the hock extends while the stifle is flexing. This provides for strong stabilization of the hock joint while the powerful gluteus and hamstrings are driving the leg back. Again, I cannot get into the complicated details, but it is important to realize that, as the rearleg is driving back, the stifle is flexing somewhat while the hock is extending. This mech-

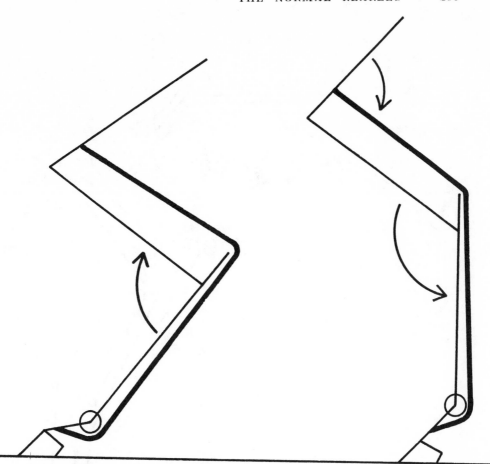

Fig. 131. This diagram illustrates how the superficial flexor (heavy, dark line) is relaxed as the hock extends, allowing the pastern to elevate. During the first part of the stride (left), the stifle and hock flex as the pastern moves down. During the second part of the stride (right), the hock extends as the stifle is flexing. This allows the pastern to elevate.

anism (stifle flexing and hock extending) permits the pastern to elevate, as it must, toward the end of the stride, by taking tension off the superficial flexor tendon (Fig. 131). This is basic to understanding tearing of the superficial flexor of the rearleg as I shall discuss later. Also, this mechanism allows the pastern to rise while at the same time not requiring that the rearquarters be lifted vertically, against the force of gravity. The horse needs to lift his front end in order to fly through the air before the next stride, but that lifting would be wasted motion for the rearleg. Therefore, the rearleg is designed to push the

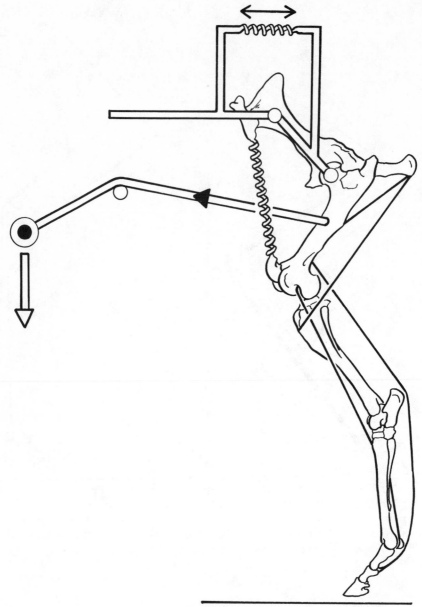

Fig. 132.   Model of the rearleg.

body forward, parallel to the ground, while the foreleg both pushes and lifts.

The function of the suspensory, digit, and so on, are essentially the same in the rearleg as in the foreleg. There are some fine points of difference, but they would make our story much too complicated.

It is time now to build another model (Fig. 132). For the really handy, try the model shown in Fig. 133. With this one, we have put the fore and rearlegs together and added the center of gravity. This one will take some doing: getting the right weight for the center of gravity, the proper size springs, elastic bands, and so forth.

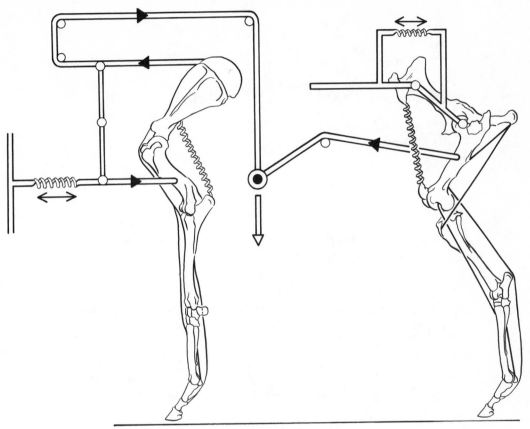

Fig. 133. Combined foreleg and rearleg model.

4

THE ABNORMAL
REARLEG

THE DIAGNOSIS OF LAMENESS IN THE REARLEG IS CONSIDERABLY MORE difficult than in the foreleg. Certain lamenesses are quite clear, readily diagnosed, and understood; but there are undoubtedly some "high" lamenesses, in the upper part of the leg, which we have not yet recognized nor defined. That is a shortcoming which we are forced to accept at the present time. With time and work perhaps we will learn more.

SACROILIAC

One identified problem is luxation, or dislocation of the sacroiliac joint. This joint is the only articulation between the vertebral column or backbone and the pelvis. Fig. 134 is an example of a horse with such a luxation. It may occur on both sides but usually appears only on one side. Interestingly enough, this lesion occurs most commonly in hunter-jumper horses and is common enough that horsemen call it a *hunter bump*. It certainly is the mark of a hunter, often a good one. He has jumped enough fences to hurt himself! The initial onset of signs may be pain and reluctance to use the leg. The animal short strides and may refuse to jump. The pain subsides but a permanent limitation of normal leg movement may remain. One must note, however, that a number of such animals go back to jumping very well. The horse in Fig. 134 was a champion hunter, steeplechaser in Australia before and after he earned his "bump." Fig. 135 shows the mechanics of development of this luxation. When the horse lands from

168

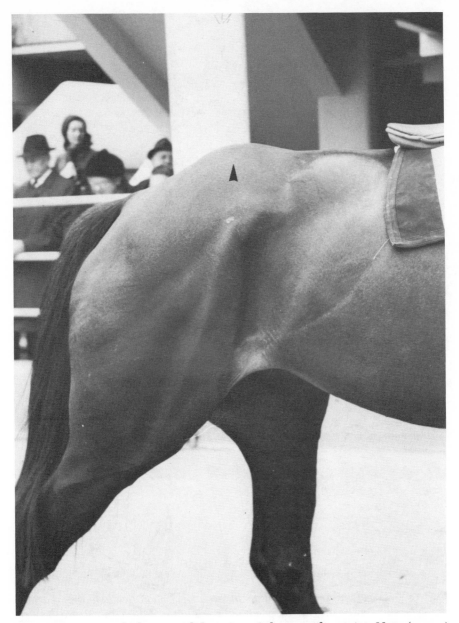

Fig. 134. A steeplechaser with luxation of the sacroiliac joint. Note (arrow) the prominence near the front part of the croup.

a jump, the rearfoot may contact the ground too far forward or slide forward as indicated by the arrow. The entire body is being supported by the one rearleg. The body weight (center of gravity) is swinging

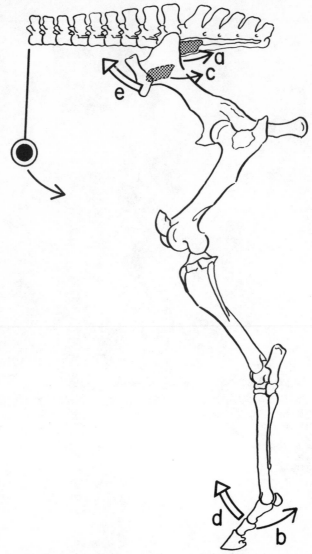

Fig. 135. *Mechanics of sacroiliac luxation. Normally, when the rearfoot impacts, the center of gravity is swinging down, rotating the sacral half of the sacroiliac in the direction of arrow a. The leg is immediately moving back (arrow b), so that the iliac half of the sacroiliac joint is rotating in the same direction (arrow c) as the sacral half. If the foot impacts too far forward, or slides forward, the leg is moving in the direction of arrow d. This means that the iliac half of the sacroiliac joint is rotating as arrow e. Since a, the sacral half, and e, the iliac half, are moving in opposite directions, the ligaments are twisted and torn and luxation occurs.*

down, as shown. The swinging down of the body causes the sacral half of the sacroiliac joint to rotate counterclockwise (the arrow, *a*). The movement of the leg sliding forward, or, in effect, being too far forward, causes the iliac half of the joint to rotate clockwise, in the opposite direction (arrow, *e*). This twisting tears the ligaments on the front of the joint allowing the pelvis, specifically the tuber sacrale, to move up and forward, producing the obvious bump. The obvious hunter's bump . . . then, is the tuber sacrale, pushed up and forward from its normal position because the ligaments have been torn. Normally, the rearleg would be moving in the opposite direction, as shown in Fig 135 and the two parts of the joint surface would be rotating in the same direction, that is, counterclockwise (*a* and *c*), and tearing would not occur.

Similar conditions can, of course, be set up when the horse crouches down to prepare for takeoff into the jump. All that is required is that the rearleg be too far forward, or moving forward, or even in proper position but with the body moving down too much or too fast (weight and fatigue), in order to cause improper twisting of the sacroiliac joint.

It may be reasonable that too great movement of the rearleg to the rear, particularly in harness horses (hiking), may be the cause of dislocation of the sacroiliac in the opposite direction, down and back, but we have no direct proof of this at the present time.

There is no treatment; just wait a while, and then bring the horse gradually back to work.

TROCHANTERIC BURSITIS

This is an acute inflammation of the bursa that lies between the attachment of one of the main tendons of the gluteus medius, the big muscle forming the croup, one of the main drivers of the rearleg (Fig. 136), and the greater trochanter of the femur. This bursa may be damaged by excessive compression when the leg is moved, protracted, too far forward. The lameness is characterized by inward rotation of the leg, dog trotting or moving away from the lame side (carrying the rear end to the side away from the pain) and a shortened forward phase (protraction) of the stride. The horse tends to carry the leg toward the midline while the foot is in the air and to go wide when the foot is on the ground. All of these signs are evidence that the animal is trying to avoid pressure on the bursa. He will also short-stride, not bring the leg as far forward, in order to avoid pain.

This lesion probably develops because the leg either slips forward on bad going, or because the horse is trying to go too fast at the trot

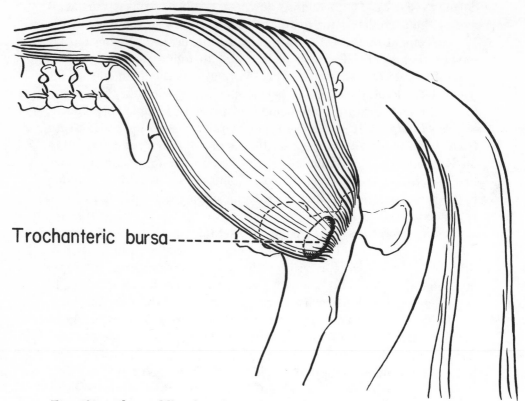

Trochanteric bursa

Fig. 136. The middle gluteal muscle attaching to the upper end of the femur with the trochanteric bursa between the attachment of the muscle and the bone.

or pace. The horse must swing the rearleg far enough forward in order to be able to swing it back fast enough to match or exceed the forward speed of the body. The faster he tries to go, the further forward he must bring the leg in order to gain the necessary angular acceleration backward. The galloping horse has little problem doing this because both rearlegs are off the ground at the same time, and he can flex his back at the lumbosacral joint, tucking his rear end under his body. You have all seen this in the galloping horse. The racing trotter or pacer cannot flex the lumbosacral joint in this manner, however, because the two rearlegs are always moving in opposite directions. At high speeds, then, he must flex his hip joint more than the runner, and the more he flexes the hip joint the more pressure he puts on the trochanteric bursa. It is not surprising that this type of lameness, in this day and time, is most common in harness horses.

It has been said that trochanteric bursitis always accompanies spavin. While this may be true, I have no pathologic evidence to support the idea, or to deny it.

Rest will often permit the bursitis—afflicted horse to return to normal. If your veterinarian can get into the bursa with a long needle (not easy to do) and inject a small amount of steroid (one time only!) the condition may rectify itself that much sooner. A major problem is to differentiate this condition from spavin, and that may be difficult. The spavin test, flexing the rearleg and trotting the horse off, should be negative with trochanteric bursitis, on the average, and positive with spavin. I should think that pulling the rearleg forward, at the same time rotating it outward, would exaggerate the trochanteric pain, but many horses resent this normally, and, therefore, the test is difficult to interpret.

HIP JOINT

This joint is rarely the site of any significant problems. Occasionally the hip is destroyed by infection with a permanently lame horse as a result. Even more rarely the two ligaments of the hip joint may be torn loose by a fall with permanent lameness thereafter. Most hip lamenesses are the result of pelvic fractures through the hip joint. Much to no one's surprise, I am sure, these rare cases present clinical signs very similar, in fact almost identical, to those of trochanteric bursitis; they are only inches apart after all.

FIBROTIC MYOPATHY

This interesting condition was described by Dr. O. R. Adams of Colorado in rodeo horses, working stock horses, horses fighting a sideline (the rear foot connected to a loop around the neck by a length of rope), or in animals that catch their rear foot in their own halter. Diagnosis is quite easy. When the foot is retracted, just before it hits the ground, it is jerked back a few inches. The lesion is a tearing followed by fibrosis (healing) of the semitendinosus muscle (Fig. 137). When the foot is sliding forward on the ground, as in a sliding stop, or when held by a side line or halter, and the big thigh muscles are contracting strongly to pull the leg back, tearing of the semitendinosus muscle may occur. This muscle, rather than one of the other two big thigh muscles, is torn because it is attached farthest from the center of rotation of the stifle joint, thus a greater moment arm = greater force.

Treatment may be conservative. Wait and see, but surgical excision of the area is usually necessary. Recovery is generally uneventful.

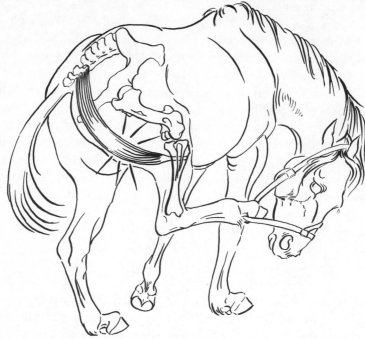

Fig. 137. This figure illustrates one way that a horse can tear the semi-tendinosus muscle (the only muscle shown).

STIFLE LAMENESS

This large, important joint is frequently blamed for lameness in the rearleg, but there is very little evidence that it really is at fault in most cases. Infectious arthritis, fractures of the patella, and avulsions of the cruciate ligaments do occur and cause exquisitely painful lameness, but they are quite rare.

Quite often the diagnosis *loose stifle* or *loose patella* is made. Such a diagnosis is arrived at by watching the horse walk and by walking him with a hand on the patella. The large quadriceps muscles seem loose and flabby, bouncing around while the patella moves up and down unevenly. I have never seen lesions at autopsy associated with this apparent looseness. In my opinion, and it is not mine alone, this looseness is simply evidence of lack of muscle condition. The horse has not worked enough to tone the quadriceps sufficiently to prevent this floppy, loose appearance. Careful training will usually "cure" this looseness.

UPWARD FIXATION — PATELLA

A real entity and a cause of gait abnormality associated with the stifle is the condition known as *upward fixation of the patella*. The horse has a unique, and normal, mechanism for resting the hindleg, as everyone knows. He hooks his patella over the inside femoral trochlea and can thereby keep the stifle from flexing without muscular effort (Fig. 138). The stifle is interconnected with the hock joint by a reciprocal mechanism: peroneus tertius, tibialis cranialis on the front and the gastrocnemius, superficial flexor tendon on the back as described earlier. When the stifle is held fixed by the hooked patella, the hock cannot flex. Since neither of the joints can flex when the patella is hooked over the inside ridge, the horse can stand with a minimum of muscular exertion.

Fixation of the patella is, then, a desirable thing, if the horse does it when he wants to. It is quite undesirable to hook the patella, however, when he is walking, trotting, or running. In order to hook the patella in this fashion, the stifle joint must be extended. Horses, and particularly ponies, with straight hindlegs are particularly prone to this inadvertent locking or fixing. The normal horse has a stifle angle of about 135°; when the stifle is extended to 143–145° the patella hooks over the inside ridge. The straight-legged pony or horse may have a stifle angle closer to 140° than 135°, and, therefore, even a slight misstep may move it the additional 3–5° and cause fixation, inadvertently.

Even horses with normal stifle angles can inadvertently fix the patella in this manner because of inadequate muscle tone ("loose" stifle) or because the foot slips forward (which tends to extend the stifle). The straight leg conformation is distinctly predisposing, however. In order to unlock, the hip and stifle should be extended as much as possible while the patella is pulled outward. Given a straight-legged horse there are only two approaches to long-term prevention of recurrence: working the animal carefully to build up his muscle tone and strength, and/or surgical division of the medial (inside) patellar ligament (which, with the patella, does the hooking). Needless to say the former is preferable to the latter since, after cutting the ligament, the horse can no longer rest the hindleg normally.

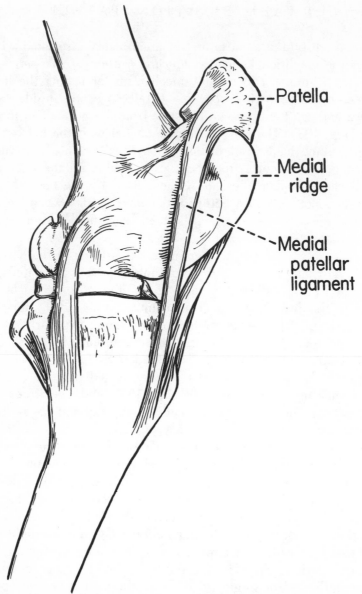

Fig. 138. The dissected stifle showing the patella hooked over the medial ridge (inside ridge of the femoral trochlea).

OSTEOCHONDROSIS

This is an extraordinarily interesting condition of essentially unknown cause. It occurs in many different joints and in many different

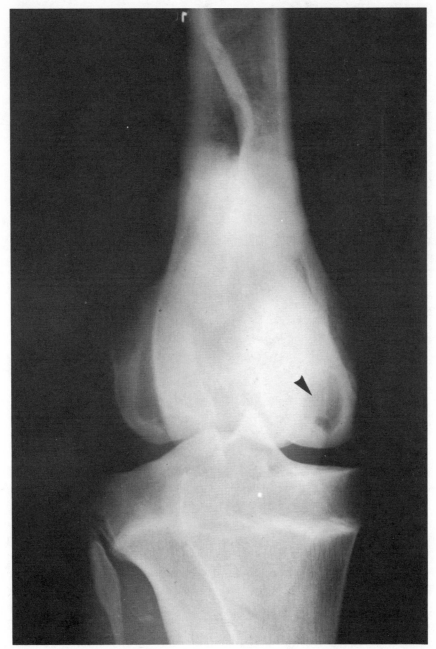

Fig. 139. "Subchondral cyst" in medial femoral condyle, front view.

species. Specifically in the stifle joint, we may see it in either of two places: the medial (inside) femoral condyle or on one of the ridges

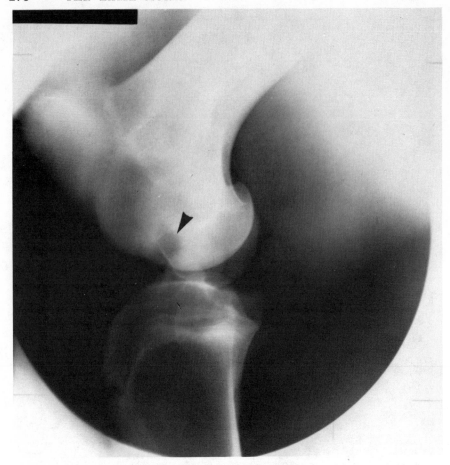

Fig. 140. Side view of Fig. 139.

of the femoral trochlea (Figs. 139–142), the former being the more frequent. It is notable that precisely the same lesion occurs in the human and in exactly the same place, the medial femoral condyle. The lesion is a partially separated piece of bone and cartilage or an area of bone loss just beneath the cartilage. The evidence, to date, suggests that most of these develop as separate ossification centers, as we discussed with the navicular bone and the proximal sesamoids. That does not help too much because in most cases we cannot explain why there should be a secondary ossification center in the first place. For present purposes, however, we can say that most of these lesions are of little importance as a cause of lameness. Occasionally, in the femoral condyle, in particular, the lesion is so large that it not only

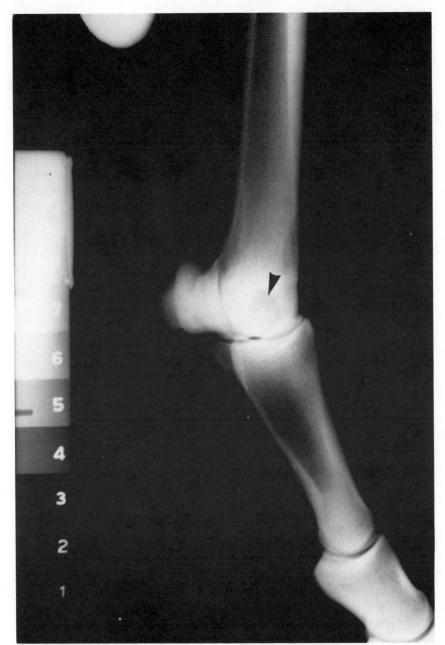

Fig. 141. A subchondral cyst in the lower end of the cannon bone.

can be seen on the X-ray, it is even the cause of lameness! Your veterinarian will want to inject anesthetic into the joint to be sure that what is seen on the X-ray is, indeed, the cause of the lameness. Rest and

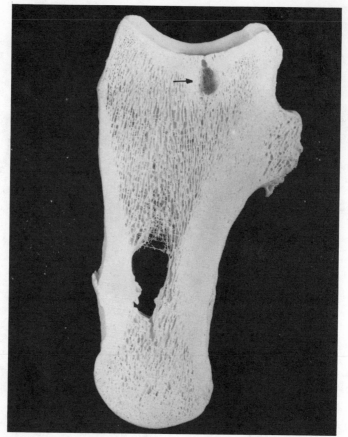

Fig. 142.   A long pastern bone with a subchondral bone defect.

mild exercise seem to be the things to do with these, but surgical intervention may be necessary if the lameness persists.

LUXATION OF THE PATELLA

This condition seems to have increased in frequency during the past few years. Most of the cases we have seen to date have been in Standardbreds, although it is seen very commonly in Holland in Shetland ponies. It may be unilateral or bilateral. All but two of the cases which have been reported have involved a slipping of the patella to the outside. This occurs because the lateral ridge of the femoral trochlea (Figs. 143, 144) is hypoplastic (did not develop properly), and the patella has no choice but to slip off. No treatment should be attempted. The chances are very good that this is an inherited condition. Affected animals should be destroyed.

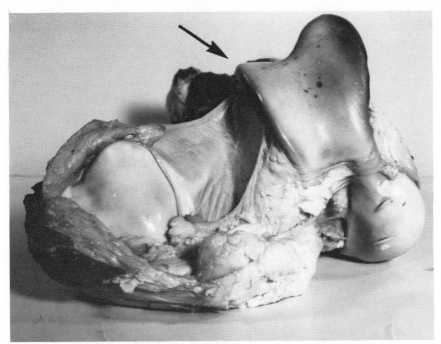

Fig. 143. *Femoral trochlea showing normal, large medial ridge and normal lateral ridge (arrow). Patella is reflected to the left.*

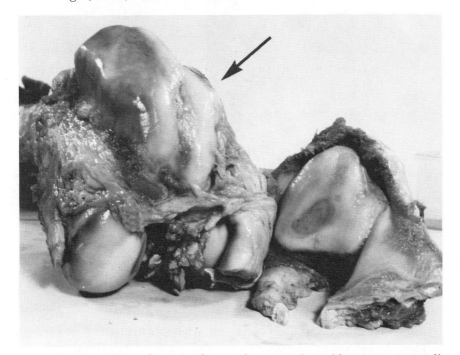

Fig. 144. *Hypoplastic lateral ridge of the femoral trochlea (arrow). Patella reflected to the right.*

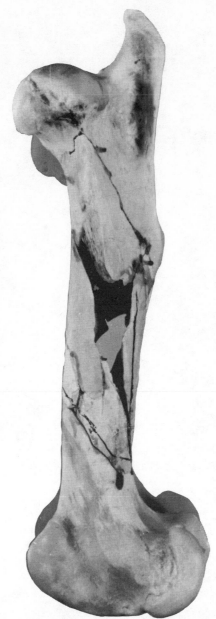

Fig. 145. Multiple fracturing of the femur.

FRACTURE—FEMUR

Fractures of the femur do occur but are not, fortunately, as common as many other types of fracture. In our present state of knowledge, and for a long time to come, such fractures are disasters (Figs. 145, 146). Only in young foals can one even hope for surgical repair.

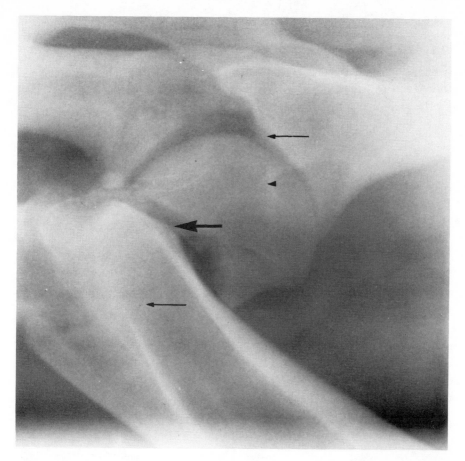

Fig. 146. Fracture of the neck of the femur. The upper arrow indicates the acetabulum, that part of the hip joint formed by the ,pelvic bones. The arrowhead indicates the head of the femur. The large arrow is the fracture through the neck of the femur. The lower, small arrow indicates the shaft of the femur.

FIBULAR "FRACTURE"

This was a favorite diagnosis for obscure rearleg lameness at one time—favorite, that is, because the so-called fractures were readily seen on X-rays. In this case as in many others, just because something different can be seen on an X-ray does not mean that it is abnormal. In fact the fibula, like the ulna, is, in part, a rudimentary bone in the horse. The upper and lower ends remain as structural and functional units. The upper end of the fibula provides for some muscular attachments, and the lower end forms part of the tibiotarsal (hock) joint.

The middle portion of the bone, however, is either completely or partially gone. As a rule only a fibrous band persists which may ossify, form bone, to one degree or another. When seen on an X-ray, incomplete, segmental ossifications may appear as fractures, but they are not fractures. So far as we know at the present time, the fibula never is the site of lesions that cause lameness.

TIBIAL FRACTURE

Fractures of the tibia (Figs. 147–149) are not uncommon. While the prognosis is not good, careful, diligent surgery and nursing may save some horses.

TIBIAL CREST AVULSIONS

The tibial tuberosity is a large prominence on the upper, front end of the tibia which serves as the point of attachment for the three patellar ligaments. It forms from a separate ossification center, so that in young horses a radiolucent line is apparent. In the human this tuberosity is sometimes avulsed, torn loose, presumably by excessive pull of the quadriceps muscles acting through the patella and, in man, the one patellar ligament. This condition, known as Osgood-Schlatter disease, has been diagnosed in young horses, probably without justification. I have never seen a bona fide case, and every suspected case I have seen was not.

SPAVIN

The word *spavin* possibly derives from the German word *spat*, and I have no idea of its derivation. There are numerous synonyms: spavin, bone spavin, jack, jack spavin, bog spavin, and blood spavin. Several different entities are represented in these terms, and I shall discuss them all.

The major entity—jack, jack spavin, bone spavin—is an arthrosis of one or both of the two lower sets of joints that comprise the hock. The hock is a complex joint like the carpus, Fig. 150. The uppermost and largest joint is formed by the lower end of the tibia and a moderate-sized bone, the tibiotarsal bone. Most of the swinging, flexion, and extension movement of the hock occurs at this joint.

The tibiotarsal bone is joined in back to a prominent bone—the tuber calcis—which forms the point of the hock and to which the gaskin muscles attach. This tuber calcis is the same bone that forms

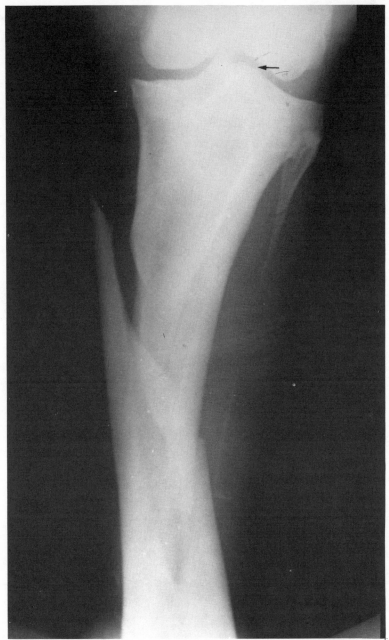

Fig. 147. Fracture of the tibia. Arrow is in the stifle joint.

Fig. 148. Fracture of the tibia.

Fig. 149. Fracture of the tibia.

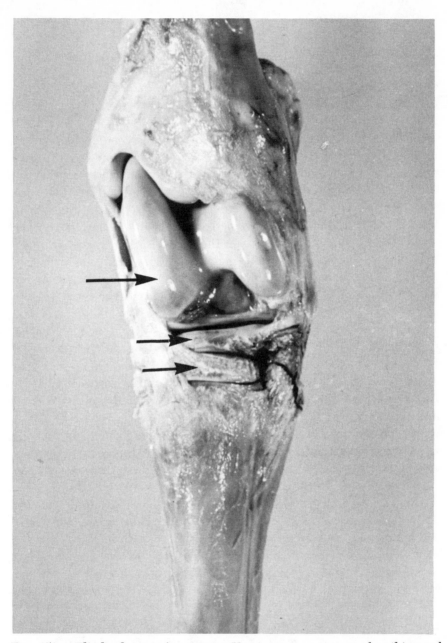

Fig. 150. The hock joint, front view. Upper arrow points to the tibiotarsal bone that articulates above with the tibia. Middle arrow indicates the central tarsal bone. Lower arrow indicates the third tarsal bone. The latter articulates below with the cannon bone.

the human heel, and, in fact, the hock joint of the horse corresponds to the ankle joint of man.

Moving down, the tibiotarsal bone forms a narrow, tight joint with the central tarsal bone. The central, in turn, forms a joint with the third tarsal bone. The third, finally, forms a joint with the upper end of the cannon bone. A number of bones have been ignored. We need only consider those bones which are apparent when viewing the hock from in front.

Why such a complex of joints? As previously noted, the upper, tibiotarsal joint provides for the wide range of flexion and extension needed for developing propulsion by the rearleg. The central and third tarsal bones and joints do not move very much. However, it is important to note that they *do move*. There has been a tendency in the past to consider these movements unimportant because they are small. The frequency of disease in these small joints, however, makes it perfectly obvious that, small or not, they are vitally important.

The small bones and joints serve two major functions. As the weight of the horse is applied to the rearleg, and the great muscles of the croup begin to drive the rearleg back—propelling the animal forward—these small bones move one on the other into the close-packed position. In this position the several bones fit together virtually perfectly and the joint is rendered immovable. In this close-packed or locked position the hock is best able to sustain the forces applied by the weight of the horse and the powerful pull of the massive croup and thigh muscles.

An analogy may be helpful. When jogging along slowly, or walking, in a jog cart, the driver may have one foot out of the stirrup, swinging loosely and comfortably. As soon as some speed is attained, however, that foot is placed firmly in the stirrup. At slow speeds the driver is balanced well enough with one or even both feet dangling. As soon as the horse accelerates, however, the driver must move to a more stable position—feet in stirrups. Similarly, the small hock joints move to a more stable, close-packed, position as soon as there is significant acceleration. The force the joint must sustain is a product of the total weight (a function of mass) and the acceleratory movement. Therefore, acceleration and, particularly, increase in acceleration is associated with increasing force.

Simply, the faster a horse goes, the greater is the acceleration, and, hence, the greater the force being applied. It is well-known that fast horses get hurt and slow horses do not (as a rule of thumb). This is surely obvious since the slow horse accelerates less, therefore the total force is smaller on his bones and joints.

Having provided some background on the normal function of the hock joint, we may now proceed to learn a bit about bone spavin. This condition is, essentially, an arthrosis of the joint between the central tarsal (TC) and third tarsal bones (T3) or the joint between T3 and the cannon bone, or both (Figs. 151–156).

It is a general rule that whenever one looks at damaged living tissue there are two processes going on at the same time: destruction and repair. As soon as tissue, cartilage, skin, liver, whatever, is destroyed or damaged a repair process starts. In studying arthrosis of the hock joint, then, we must be concerned with both of these processes.

As the cartilage is worn away, the neighboring tissues attempt to repair the damage. New blood vessels grow into the cartilage from the underlying bone, converting the cartilage into bone as they grow.

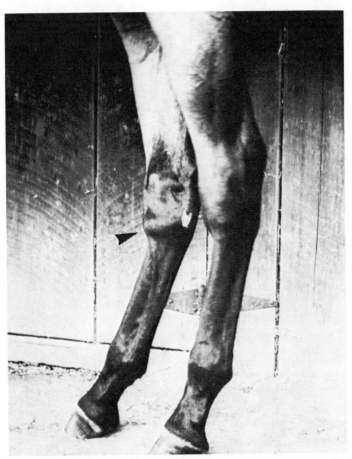

Fig. 151.   Large bone spavin on the inside of the right hock.

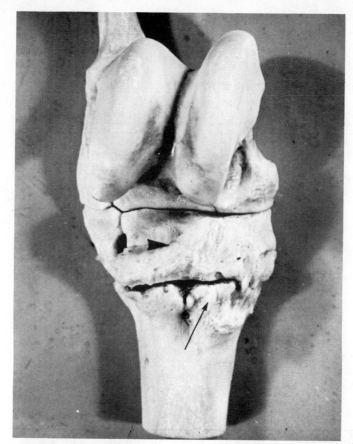

Fig. 152. *Front view of spavin involving both the central tarsal-third tarsal joint and the third tarsal-cannon bone joint. Arrow is pointing at the latter.*

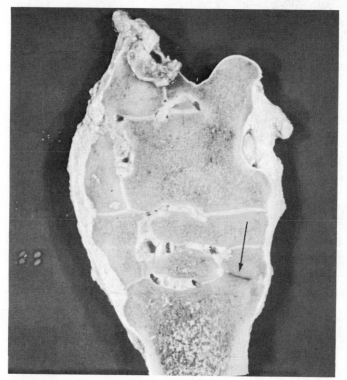

Fig. 153. *A sawed section of the hock showing spavin involving only the third tarsal-cannon bone joint (arrow pointing to the dark, damaged cartilage).*

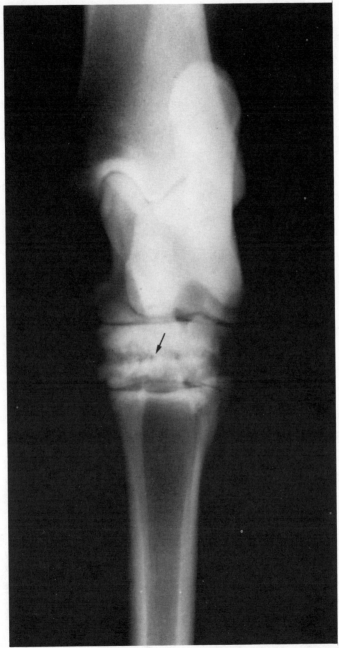

Fig. 154.   Front view radiograph with the arrow pointing to spavin of the central tarsal-third tarsal joint.

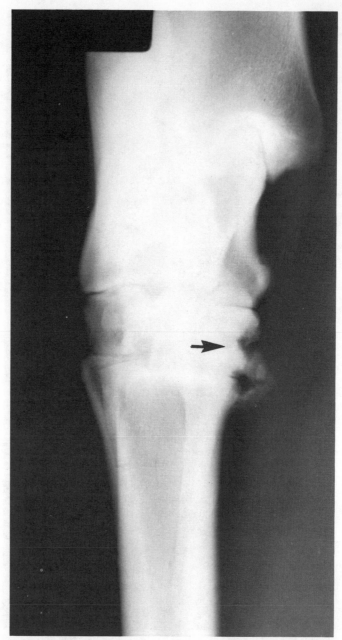

Fig. 155. Front view radiograph. Arrow points to the central tarsal-third tarsal spavin. There is, also, spavin of the third tarsal-cannon bone joint (just below the arrow).

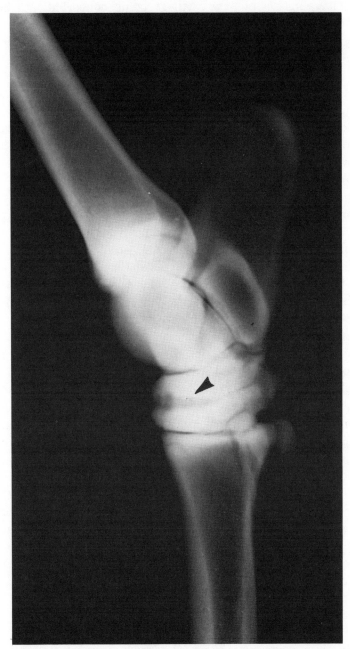

Fig. 156. Side view. Arrow points to spavin of the central tarsal-third tarsal joint. The third tarsal-cannon bone joint is normal.

The undamaged cartilage begins to grow at the same time and very soon we have masses of new cartilage being converted into bone all around the damaged joint. These new bone masses, osteophytes, show up very strikingly on X-rays of the joint. They are frequently called *calcium deposits* around the joint but they are not, as I have said before. They are masses of new bone.

An important point needs to be made here. When the joint is first damaged, there is pain, and the horse will be lame. X-rays at this time, however, generally will not show any changes in or around the involved joint. The eroding cartilage is radiolucent, that is, does not show on the X-ray plate, and it is extremely difficult to tell if it is damaged. Once the repair process begins, the osteophytes start to grow and these new spicules of bone can be seen on the X-ray plate. Therefore, when changes appear on the X-ray, the disease process is well advanced. While X-ray films are of great help, they are not the whole answer to any given diagnostic problem.

Earlier I mentioned that bone spavin may involve either one or both of the small hock joints. In the harness horse, as well as in draft horses and hunters, the disease usually starts in the joint between TC and T3. When spavin occurs in running horses, and it is very uncommon, it starts in the T3-cannon bone joint.

Why is this? The answer, unfortunately, is quite complex. Boiling down to essentials, the TC-T3 damage occurs in those horses which habitually work with the hock joint in a markedly bent or flexed position. Both the harness horse and draft horse must pull a load behind them. In order to do this efficiently they lower the croup, thereby increasing the propulsive force exerted by their rearlegs. In lowering the croup, however, they must inevitably flex the hock. Man does the same thing. If you are trying to push or pull a heavy object along the ground, you squat down, closing ankle, knee, and hip joint angles in order to increase the force you can exert against the ground. The hunter, similarly, must lower his croup, flexing the hock, in order to generate sufficient force to get up and over jumps.

Now, there is a type of conformation that corresponds to this flexed hock position and you all know it: sickle hock. Unfortunately, a great many harness horses tend to be sickle-hocked to some degree and, therefore, are predisposed to the development of spavin.

Why are so many harness horses sickle-hocked? For the same reason that many draft horses are (or were). That is, man selects for breeding purposes those animals best able to do the job that man wants done. Man wants fast harness horses. A fast harness horse, a winner, must be able to pull a load efficiently. The most efficient confrontation for that purpose is sickle hock. Therefore, man inadvertently selects for the sickle conformation when selecting the best racehorse for the breeding ranks.

Once the spavin begins, the cartilage is damaged, and pain appears, the horse develops a characteristic shortening of the stride of the affected rearleg in an attempt to relieve the pain. In so doing, however, he may damage the other joint, between T3 and the cannon bone. Damage here, as I mentioned, typically occurs in runners, and most of our better runners today tend to be straight legged behind. It is clear that a horse that is short-striding is functionally straight legged. Our initially sickle-hocked horse, either functionally or by conformation, develops TC-T3 damage. The pain causes him to short-stride, converting him to a straight-legged way of going. That, in turn, leads to T3-cannon bone damage if he continues to race or work. Thus is it that in older harness horses we tend to see damage involving both the hock joints.

Among harness horses it is also true that trotters tend to spavin somewhat more than pacers. (With so few trotters as compared to pacers in this day and time, one might not be able to detect that without statistical studies.) This is simply because the trotter tends to go wider behind than the pacer. On the same count the cow-hocked horse tends to spavin more than a normal horse. In effect cow hock is the same thing as sickle hock except in a different plane. In other words the wide-going trotter is the functional equivalent of the conformational cow-hock.

How does one prevent or treat spavin? Prevention, I guess, is impossible. If we are to use draft horses, race harness horses, and jump horses, spavin is inevitable. We cannot prevent it; we can only live with it. The best recourse probably is to keep going with the horse, using pain-killers as necessary, to encourage ankylosis of the small tarsal joints. In other words keep the damage to the joints going until they have nothing else to do but fuse together. The pain will then disappear and the horse can go on. Surgical fusion techniques have been developed. At this juncture I do not know if they are any better than pain-killers and continued work. Given the way surgical procedures are evaluated (see carpus) in horse medicine, I doubt that we shall ever know the answer. Cunean tenotomy is frequently employed. Often it is justified on the grounds that there is inflammation of the bursa between the tendon and the underlying tissues, a structure quite separate from the hock joints themselves. I have never seen such a bursitis and do not believe that it exists. Cunean tenotomy, however, does remove one pull on the tarsal bones and thereby could encourage fusion.

It is generally true that a horse lame in one leg can become secondarily lame in another leg. That is, he is just sore enough to hurt but able to keep going, transferring some of the load from the sore leg to another leg. Because of this increased loading of the previously normal leg, we may expect the development of a lesion in that leg. There are a number of examples of this sort of thing which one could cite. I shall mention two here. I have seen a number of cases of damage to the suspensory ligament of the foreleg which, after rest, seemed to come sound. When returned to hard training, however, the pain was still present; the animal tried to shift the load to the opposite foreleg, overdorsiflexed the fetlock joint as a result, and fractured the sesamoid bones.

Horses developing spavin, and they usually damage both hocks, may try to shift their weight forward onto the forelegs, trying to relieve their painful hocks. Such animals can develop navicular disease because of this overloading of the forelegs. Precisely the same thing can happen, in reverse, when navicular disease is the primary problem. The animal tries to take the load off the forelegs by camping under, keeping the hindfeet further forward under the body. This obviously makes him functionally sickle hocked and that, of course, leads to spavin.

BOG SPAVIN

Bog spavin is a distension (swelling) of the tibiotarsal joint, the large upper joint of the hock, by increased amounts of synovial fluid. This is a common condition. It is rarely, if ever, associated with lameness and, at the worst, constitutes a blemish that upsets beauty contest judges. It appears that osteochondrosis (see below) may sometimes be associated with the increased amount of synovial fluid. Often there are small erosions on the front edges of the lower end of the tibia and the corresponding surfaces of the tibiotarsal bone. It is obvious that these two surfaces only come into contact during extreme flexion of the hock and that only happens when the foot is off the ground. The cause of these small erosions is probably the extreme flexion such as is seen, and encouraged, in gaited horses, Hackney ponies, Tennessee Walkers, etc. Bog spavin is not associated with lameness because the two damaged surfaces only come into contact when the foot is off the ground, unloaded, and only for the brief moment of extreme flexion. As a general rule, lameness pain arises from contact of damaged surfaces when loaded, foot on the ground, and not when the leg is unloaded, foot off the ground.

BLOOD SPAVIN

This is merely the saphenous vein over the inside of the hock. It is normal.

OSTEOCHONDROSIS

Quite often, at autopsy, we find a small piece of partially loose bone (Figs. 157–159) at the front edge of the median ridge of the lower end of the tibia, within the tibiotarsal joint. The cause of this separate piece of bone is not known. We do know, however, that it is quite common, very often bilateral (in both legs) and, as far as

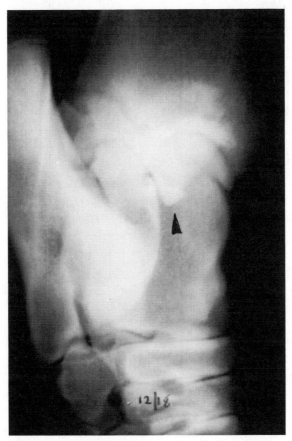

Fig. 157. Oblique view showing (arrow head) the separate piece of bone in the tibiotarsal joint.

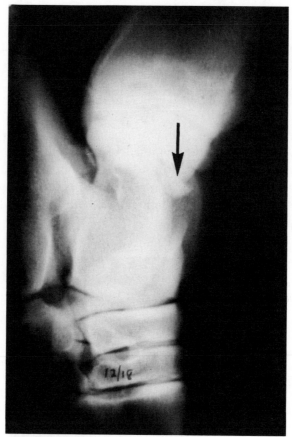

Fig. 158.   Lateral view of Fig. 157.

can be determined, rarely if ever associated with lameness. Referring to what was said above, this should be clear because there is no way for this piece of bone to come in contact with any other part of the hock except during extreme flexion of the hock joint. Unfortunately, this piece can often be seen on X-rays; ergo, it is blamed for lameness, and surgery is performed to remove the "fracture." If you are going to radiograph one hock for suspected lameness always radiograph the other. You will quickly decide that since the same "lesion" is present in both sides there is not much point in removing this innocuous piece of bone. It is not normal, but it does not appear to be harmful.

One of the ridges of the tibiotarsal bone may also be the site for an osteochondrosis lesion. Again, it is of no known clinical significance.

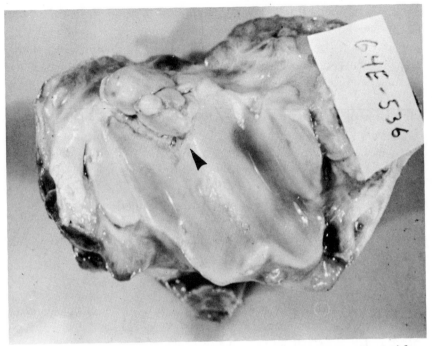

Fig. 159. The lower end of the tibia showing the separate piece of bone (arrowhead).

DRIVER WEIGHT AND THE HARNESS HORSE

I have spoken several times now about the load that the harness horse must pull behind him. Those among you who are concerned with such animals may well be scoffing. It is generally believed, and this belief has been encouraged by a variety of knowledgeable engineers, that the driver's weight has no influence on the racing harness horse. While these engineers no doubt know all there is to know about engineering, their knowledge of the horse is somewhat sparse.

As I have said previously, force is a function of acceleration:

$F = M \times A$ (force equals mass multiplied by acceleration)

Every time there is a change in acceleration, there will be a change in force, increasing or decreasing. A harness horse is moving along, pulling his load behind him. Let us say he is a pacer and that at this precise moment, the left front and left rearlegs are on the ground pushing while the right legs are being protracted. As the left legs complete their pushing the animal flies through the air before the right legs impact. For a brief moment he is flying free through the air. It can be shown that the animal is moving at a near constant velocity while both left feet are on the ground, and that there is very little acceleration. At the moment he vaults into the air, however, acceleration suddenly appears. While flying through the air, gravity and wind resistance plus the frictional resistance of the cart wheels on the ground (no matter how small) are slowing him down. He is decelerating. At the moment the right legs impact, then, the horse will be moving at his slowest. In order to regain the constant velocity, preparatory to the next leap into the air, he must accelerate again. At this point, the force increases: immediately after his right legs impact. There are, then, two points, immediately after landing and immediately before takeoff when acceleration is significant. With the appearance of acceleration, force increases, and it is at these times that the weight of the driver does have an effect.

It is true that these force changes are small at each point in time, but it is the constant repetition of these force changes over a long period of time that leads to fatigue of the articular cartilage, and that means cartilage damage: spavin. Driver weight may not affect racing speed, but it does participate in the cause of spavin!

Precisely the same reasoning applies to the jumping horse, the other major victim of spavin. This poor animal, however, must push the weight (himself and the rider) over a longer and higher flight path, and that does not change the general situation for the hock one iota. Have you noticed how the jumper gathers himself, drops his croup, to get underway again (accelerate, in other words) after he has come down from a jump? He has two periods of startling acceleration: taking off and immediately after landing.

The essence of the engineers' miscalculation, then, is that they do not know how a horse moves, and they do not know how spavin occurs. Other than that they are in fine shape. (I will make an exception for John Jackiewicz, *Hoof Beats*, December, 1971; he does not know about spavin, but he has the rest of his head together!)

GOITER

In the past, it was not uncommon to see goiters, enlarged thyroid glands, in newborn and young foals. Usually the thyroid enlargement disappears about one to two months of age. In an occasional animal, however, this enlarged gland is associated with enlarged hocks and lameness.

The story is this: thyroid hormone encourages the maturation of bones, including the small tarsal bones. If the hormone is absent or present in insufficient amounts, the tarsal bones, which are largely still cartilage at birth, do not convert to bone rapidly enough. The foal grows in weight and size, however, putting increasing load on the tarsal bones. Cartilage can withstand less load than bone, so the small tarsal bones eventually crush, leading to enlarged hocks. This is caused by excessive intake of iodine by the mare during pregnancy. Too much iodine may block the proper functioning of the fetal thyroid gland, leading to goiter and deficient thyroid hormone production. The mare's thyroid "escapes" from this block, but the foal's thyroid cannot until after birth. Kelp feeding is the worst offender. It is one of the "fad" feeds so frequently purveyed to horsemen as a cure-all, and so eagerly gobbled up by the gullible. Kelp has a very high iodine content, much more than is needed. Free choice iodized salt is all the mare needs. Let the kelp stay in the ocean where it belongs. How many horses have you seen swimming in the Pacific eating that stuff?

CURB

This is a tearing of the plantar tarsal ligament on the back of the hock. This large, strong ligament serves to resist the pull of the gastrocnemius muscle acting on the tuber calcis (Fig. 160). Curb is primarily a disease of younger horses and particularly horses that either have sickle hocks or are worked in a functionally sickle-hocked manner. The horse is lame and the acute swelling and inflammation associated with the tear is readily seen and palpated on the back, outside part of the hock.

The tearing occurs during the first part of the stride and occurs because the resistance of the foot on the ground is greater than the force of the contracting gastrocnemius (the biceps femoris also is attached, in part, to the tuber calcis and is the more powerful). Fig. 160 shows this in a very simple form. It is obviously easier for the hock to extend from position A than from position B. Mechanically, the angle of the hock in A is greater than angle in B which means that the cosine of B is greater and this means that the resistance is greater. Don't let that get you uptight; just look at the picture; mechanics is nothing but a mathematical way of saying the obvious.

I do not know that one has to do a lot about a curb other than to rest the horse for awhile, and wait for the inflammation to subside and the torn fibers to heal. Firing the area, blisters, and other such treatments will not speed healing.

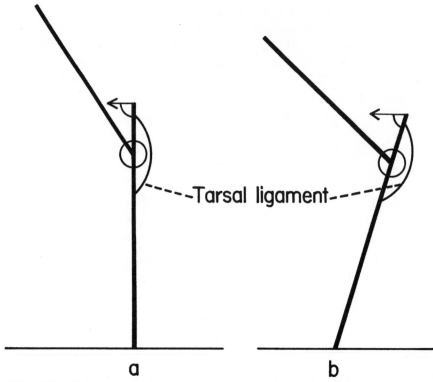

Fig. 160. Schematic of hock and curb mechanics. If the leg is in position, b, sickle-hock, the muscles must pull harder to move the leg back and the tarsal ligament may be torn.

RUPTURE—PERONEUS TERTIUS

Rupture of the peroneus tertius is not the most common of lesions, but it does occur. Figure 161 shows how this happens. There are two muscles on the front of the gaskin, the peroneus and the tibialis cranialis. Usually the peroneus tears rather than the tibialis because the peroneus has been reduced, developmentally, to virtually a ligament (like the suspensory and the superficial flexor) which is less extensible than the fleshier tibialis cranialis. One might suggest, without complete proof, that a lesser degree of rupture of the peroneus may occur and be a source of pain in the hock region, which would not be detected by the usual spavin test. This is somewhat reasonable because, as already described, the hock extends while the stifle flexes during the second half of the rearleg stride. Some X-ray evidence of new bone formation at the point of attachment of the peroneus supports this view.

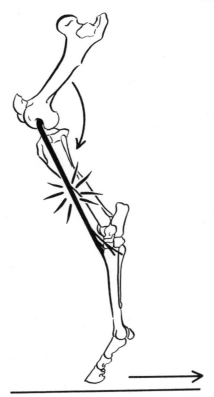

Fig. 161. Mechanics of peroneus tertius rupture. Sudden backward slipping of the leg, or the equivalent such as holding the foot back (caught in fence) with horse trying to jerk the foot free. See text.

The clinical signs of peroneus rupture are quite easy if one is aware. When the horse is walked, there will be a lag or delay in forward movement, protraction, of the leg from the hock down (Fig. 162) with the foot off the ground. One can also manipulate the leg to show that the hock can be extended without extending the stifle, which one cannot do normally. These ruptures usually repair themselves if the horse is stall-rested for about six months.

A special case of peroneus tearing carried to the ultimate extreme seems to be a problem primarily of stallions and board fences. The nervous, lonely stallion, isolated from the band of mares that nature intended him to have, may develop the habit of kicking at the fences, just for something to do, like the bored horse that takes on the long-term project of cribbing his stall to pieces. Kicking like this, the horse may catch his foot between two planks and snatch mightily to free it. This action causes flexion of the stifle but prevents flexion of the hock and, in fact, extends it. The peroneus and tibialis are ruptured and the

Fig. 162. Peroneus tertius rupture. Hock is extended while stifle is flexed. Normally, the horse cannot do this when the foot is off the ground.

hock dislocated, with or without fracture. I have seen several such cases, all in stallions. All efforts to cast and repair the damage were of no avail.

SPLINTS AND SPLINT FRACTURES

Rearleg splints and fractures are uncommon, probably because the horse carries only about forty-five percent of his body weight on the rearlegs, and because he rests one leg after the other, something he cannot do with the forelegs. The rearleg splint is almost invariably on the outside of the leg, in contrast to the foreleg, and more frequent in harness horses. This is simply because the anatomical predisposition which I mentioned with the foreleg is exactly reversed in the rearleg.

So-called blind splint (suspensory muscle damage) may occur in the rearleg.

CAPPED HOCK

There is a small bursa between the skin and the upper end of the tuber calcis similar to and for the same reason as the bursa found over the olecranon process. If the horse bangs the tuber calcis enough times against the wall, fence, or what have you, the little bursa becomes inflamed. When the bursa is inflamed and swollen, you have a capped hock. They can be very nasty to treat and are usually lifetime blemishes (see shoe boil).

BOWED TENDON

As already noted, bowed tendon, tearing of the superficial flexor tendon, is not common in the rearleg, but does occur, particularly in harness horses. The complete mechanical story of how it happens is a very nice one, but beyond our scope. I have already emphasized that the hock extends while the stifle flexes during the latter part of the propulsion movement of the rearleg. That action loosens the superficial flexor tendon, allowing it to shorten and elevate the pastern toward the end of the stride. With the conformational or functionally sickle-hocked horse, the foot may still be quite far forward when the stifle starts its normal extension toward the end of the stride. In effect the hock will be flexing while the stifle is extending, the opposite of normal (Fig. 163). This will put severe strain on the superficial flexor and tear it. Horses already sore in the front legs have a strong tendency, as already mentioned, to place the rear feet too far forward and are particularly predisposed to bowing the superficial flexor tendon of the rearleg.

SUPERFICIAL FLEXOR TENDON DISLOCATION

Another rare lesion in this area is a rupture of one or both of the attachments of the superficial flexor tendon to the tuber calcis. The tendon then slips off to one side or the other. There is nothing one can do about this. Some form of surgical repair might be feasible, but there have been so few cases that no adequate technique has as yet been developed. It is surprising that at least three of these horses have returned to work after a long rest and are presently sound.

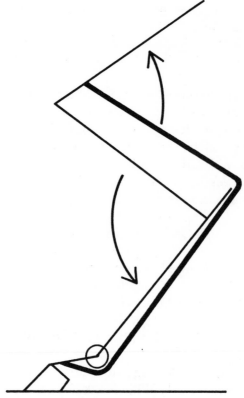

Fig. 163. The mechanism of superficial flexor tendon bowing of the rearleg. The stifle is extending and the hock is flexing, the opposite of the normal situation. The pastern cannot elevate, and the tendon is severely stretched and may be torn.

CHECK LIGAMENT

Check ligament damage in the rearleg is also very uncommon. The only mechanism for it that I can think of is shown in Fig. 164. The horse catches his toe in the ground while protracting the leg, providing the necessary snap to damage the check. The check is quite small in the rearleg as compared to the foreleg and may be absent in some animals. How embarrassing it would be to diagnose check ligament strain of the rearleg when the check is not even there! It has happened!

THOROUGHPIN

There is a tarsal synovial sheath surrounding the deep flexor tendon on its way around behind the hock just as there is a similar sheath

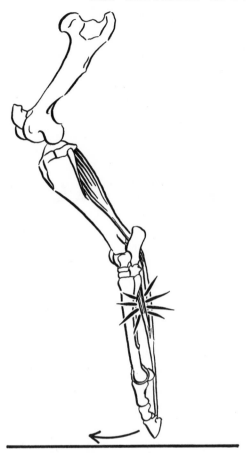

Fig. 164. Possible mechanism for rearleg check ligament damage. Toe catches the ground while the leg is protracting, snapping the check ligament.

behind the carpus. The tarsal sheath sometimes becomes distended with synovial fluid and is called, for some reason, thoroughpin. It is readily seen and palpated. I have seen very few of these at postmortem and, frankly, have no idea of what causes the increased fluid and subsequent distension of the sheath. Many of these horses are only lame for the first day or two, become sound and remain so. Treatment is usually unwarranted.

Other lesions, from the hock down, are similar to those already described for the foreleg except that they are much less common than in the foreleg. This is simply because the foreleg is primarily a supporter of fifty-five percent of the body while the rearleg is a propeller.

5

THE VERTEBRAL COLUMN

AS WITH THE FORE- AND REARLEGS WE MUST GIVE SOME CONSIDERATION to the normal functioning of the vertebral column before we can begin to consider abnormalities. The horse is galloping along, flies through the air, and lands on one rearleg; that is the total support for his body at that particular moment. Mechanically we can simplify the situation to look like Fig. 165. Since the mass of the horse, acting at the center of gravity, is tending to bend the back down, the horse's problem is to resist that bending tendency. In other words, he must provide, or be provided with, ligaments and muscles that pull the back in the other direction. As shown in Fig. 166 he has just such muscles and ligaments, and they pull the back in the direction shown.

In the figure it is apparent that the muscles are pulling at an angle relative to the vertebral column. This muscle force can be resolved into its two component forces by the use of vector analysis. That sounds complicated but it really is not. Simply put, it means that if we pull on the back (arrow u) and at the same time pull backwards (arrow s), we accomplish the same thing as pulling in the direction that the muscle is actually pulling (arrow r). Turning that around, we can say that the muscle pull, because it is on an angle to the vertebral column tends to pull that column in two directions, up and back. The purpose of the upward pull is apparent: to resist the downward effect of the center of gravity. The backward pull clearly will tend to push or crowd the individual vertebrae together against the attachments of the vertebral column to the rearleg. This

208

Fig. 165. The galloping horse has just landed on one rearleg. The bending of the back is indicated.

acts to stabilize the vertebral column, render it stiffer, more rigid. Many muscles in the body serve this double function, whether in the back or forelegs. Whenever a joint is moving, it is necessary for the muscles to both cause the movement and, at the same time, press the joints together for stability. You can test this important phenomenon on yourself: let your arm hang down loosely and move the wrist by shaking your whole arm; the wrist flops back and forth. With the arm in the same position, deliberately move your wrist. In the latter movement the muscles are working and stabilizing the wrist at the same time that they are moving it. You can accomplish a great deal more effective work in the latter case, the stable and moving wrist, than in the former case, the unstable and moving wrist.

Next the animal puts the other rearleg on the ground and, obviously, the mechanical situation does not change. Now, the first rearleg leaves the ground and the diagonal foreleg impacts, so that the horse is supported by the right rearleg and the left foreleg. The mechanical situation now changes. The animal is supported fore and rear with the center of gravity in between (Fig. 167). The center of gravity pull is in the direction of the arrow and, of course, must be resisted. How is the horse to do this? Obviously he does not and cannot have muscles

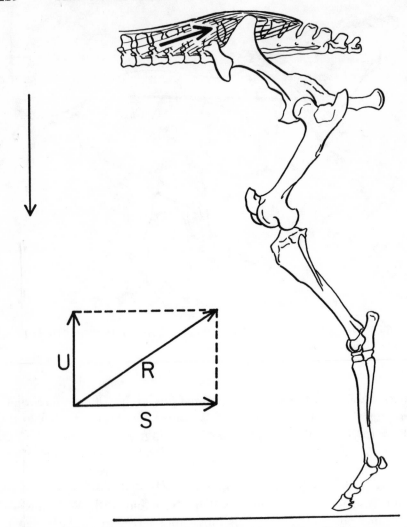

Fig. 166. The muscles (primarily the longissimus dorsi) that prevent the back from bending as shown in Fig. 165. The vertical arrow to the left is the center of gravity pulling down toward the ground. The heavy diagonal arrow, above, shows the pull of the muscles. The box, below, shows this same "muscle" arrow as the diagonal arrow, R. This muscle force, R, is composed of two other forces: U which pulls up, counteracting the downward pull of the center of gravity, and S which presses the vertebrae together, stabilizing the back.

arranged to pull straight up. In his infinite wisdom, then, the horse has his muscles arranged to do at least two things at once. The muscles we have already seen associated with the rearleg support phase pull just as they did before, up and back. At the same time muscles associated with the foreleg pull up and forward (Fig. 167). Now we take the pull of the rearleg muscles and the pull of the foreleg muscles and put them together by the very simple procedure of vector addition. The results of that addition (not surprisingly it is called a *resultant*)

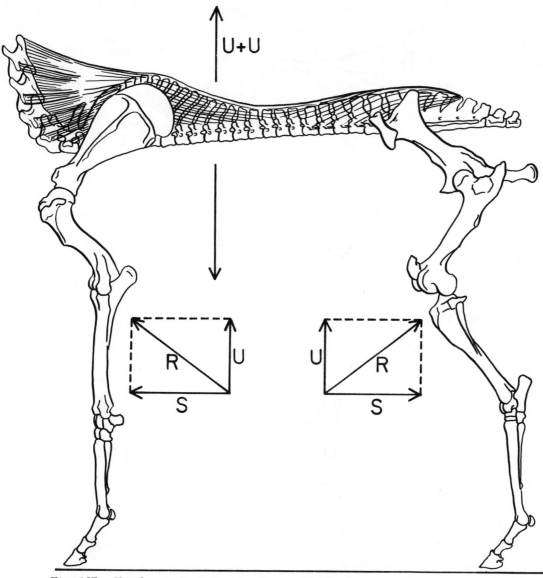

Fig. 167. Foreleg and rearleg together, with the horse standing (or supported on the diagonal during the gallop). The U and U forces combine to produce a force straight up which counteracts the vertical downward pull of gravity. The S forces stabilize the backbone; hold it together.

is a force, the u + u arrow pointing straight up. So the horse supports his backbone as the result of the muscles pulling on the fore- and rearlegs as the two points of support.

Now the right rearfoot leaves the ground and the animal is supported entirely on the left front and, shortly thereafter, the right front. I hope you see immediately what happens. Now the foreleg

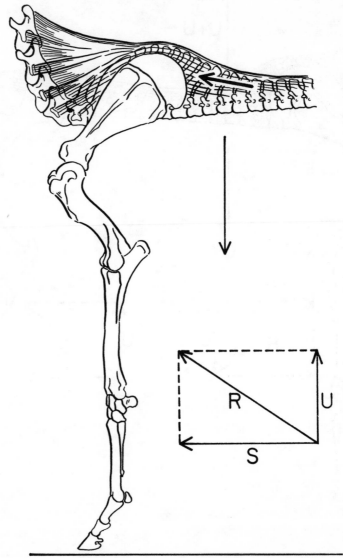

Fig. 168. The same situation as Fig. 166 but with the horse supported on the foreleg only. The arrows are the same as in Fig. 166 but pointing in the opposite direction.

muscles support and lift the body in exactly the opposite sense of the rearleg, a mirror image (Fig. 168). The musculature of the horse's back, then, supports the back in whatever the position the horse finds himself.

Let's now add in the neck for it serves a very significant and important function in locomotion. While flying through the air, and when supported by the rearlegs, the head and neck are raised. During the diagonal phase of the gallop, as the body is shifting forward from the rearlegs to the forelegs, the head and neck swing down (Fig. 169). This downswing serves to lift the rearquarters free of the ground and to pull them forward. The movement of the head and neck during the gallop, then, assists the animal to move forward. Obviously this mechanism operates much less efficiently at the trot or pace, particularly if, as with most racing trotters and pacers, the head is held up with a check rein.

It should now be apparent that a long neck is an advantage to a horse required to go fast. It is also of great advantage to a jumping horse because the downswing of the head and neck helps to lift the rearquarters over the jump. It is also the reason why the rider must let the horse have his head when jumping, so that he can use his head and neck to help get his rearquarters over the fence. There are disadvantages to the long neck, however, as we shall see shortly. In selecting for horses that run fast and jump high, man has selected for long necks, though not, perhaps, knowing why he has done so. He has also bought himself wobblers and roarers as I shall discuss below.

DISKS

Everybody knows about slipped disks in the human. They also occur in dogs and cats. They do not, however, occur in horses. The intervertebral disk (inter = between, between vertebrae; Fig. 170) is a shock absorbing pad between two adjacent vertebrae. In man and dogs it is a fibrous ring with a soft gelatinous center. It is this center that undergoes degeneration, protrudes through the outer fibrous ring, causing pressure on nerves or the spinal cord. The horse, and most other large animals, do not have disks with a soft center. The disk is almost entirely composed of tough fibrous tissue and never slips. Horses do have things wrong with their backs, but slipped disk is not one of them.

The horse's intervertebral disks do tend to degenerate, the centers disappearing with increasing age. This is particularly true of the disks

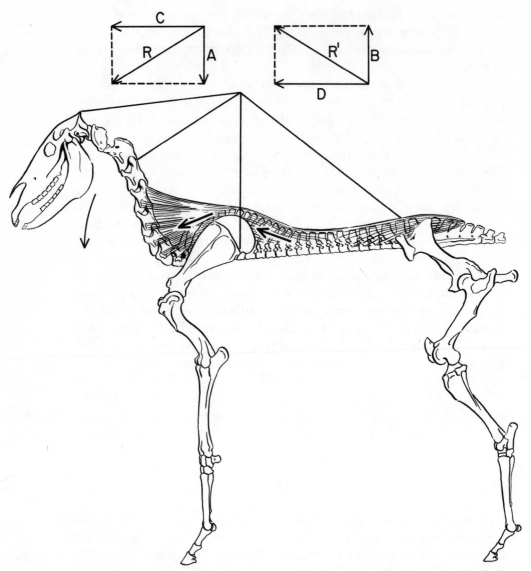

Fig. 169. *This figure illustrates how the downswing of the head and neck aids locomotion. The downswing pulls on the back and neck muscles (heavy arrows on the muscles which correspond to R and R′ in the diagram above). The down pull of R, the force A, is erased by the up pull of R′, the force B. What remains, then, are the horizontal forces, C and D, which add together to pull the horse forward, aiding locomotion.*

of the neck and at the junction of the back with the pelvis, the lumbrosacral disk. There is not much mystery about why this happens; there is more movement at these areas than any place else in the

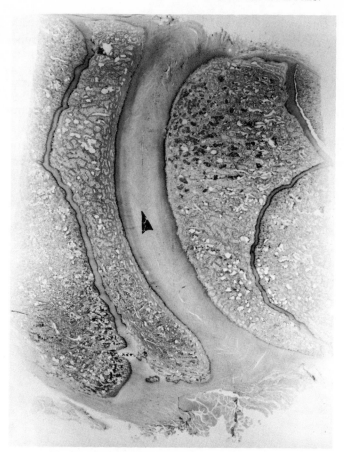

Fig. 170. Low-power magnified photograph of the intervertebral disk of a horse. The arrow head is in the center of the disk. The vertebral bodies and their epiphyseal plates are to left and right.

vertebral column, and the more you use something the quicker it wears out. This degeneration, which is invariably seen in older horses, is rarely if ever associated with any clinical problem.

CONGENITAL DEFECTS

Foals are occasionally born with scoliosis (curving to one side) of the vertebral column. I have already discussed this briefly with contractures of the legs. This curvature develops because the little articulations of the vertebral column are hypoplastic, underdeveloped, on one side, and the spine moves to that side. This is probably the same thing that causes scoliosis in many children (not all; there are other causes) but so far I do not believe it has been demonstrated.

More rarely these little articular processes will be hypoplastic, or even completely absent, on both sides at the same time. This results in a foal born with severe lordosis or sway back (Fig. 171). When hypoplastic on one side the spine moves to that side; when hypoplastic on both sides (Fig. 172) the spine moves toward the ground because of the pull of gravity toward the ground. Some very old horses also develop swayback. This is the result of a gradual deterioration and stretching of the ligaments on the ventral surface of the vertebrae combined with years of carrying his own weight around. I shall talk more about that sort of thing when I come to spondylosis deformans.

VERTEBRAL FRACTURES

Horses do break their backs and in a variety of ways, though certain types of fracture are more common than others (Figs. 173–175). There is no point to going into a long dissertation on the subject of broken backs. It is a disaster and that is that. The mechanics are interesting, including the explanation of why they almost always break in the same general area, near the twelfth thoracic vertebra. Simply

Fig. 171. Severe lordosis or swayback. The animal was born this way.

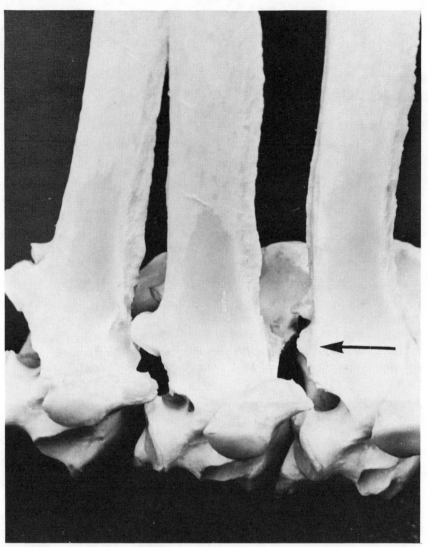

Fig. 172. Oblique view of cleaned vertebrae from the horse in Fig. 171. At the arrow the intervertebral joint processes are very small (compare to next set to the left). This leads to swayback.

put, this is because the point of greatest mobility of the horse's back (the thoracolumbar part of his back) is near the twelfth thoracic vertebra, and it is excessive movement, downward bending of the back that causes the fracture. An example of this is a spasm of the back muscles in a horse afflicted with tetanus. A few tetanus horses go down and die, or have to be destroyed, because they fracture their backs during a tetanic muscle spasm.

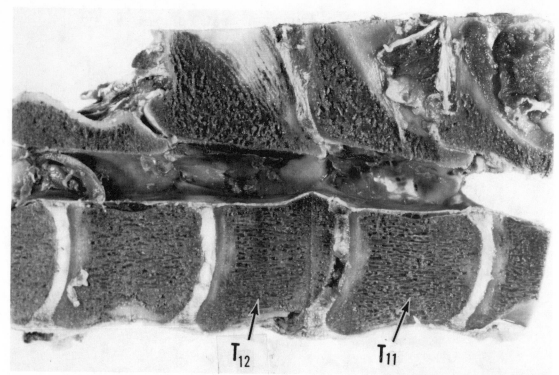

Fig. 173. *Fracture of the twelfth thoracic vertebra. The bone is crushed and bulging up into the canal that contained the spinal cord.*

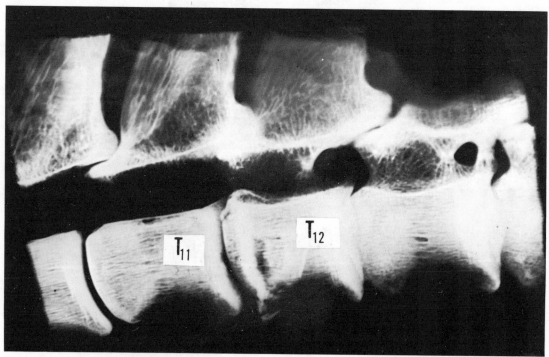

Fig. 174. *Radiograph of the specimen in Fig. 173. Note the distortion and crushing of T 12 (the dense white area running vertically to the left of the marking 'T 12').*

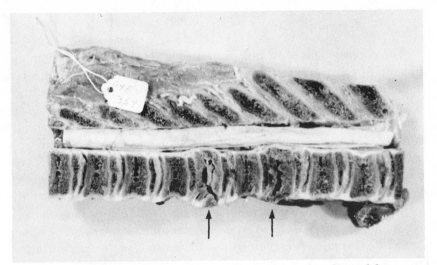

Fig. 175. Two crushed, fractured vertebrae in a foal indicated by arrows. The spinal cord (white) is in place and the damaged vertebrae can be seen pressing up against it.

The body of a vertebra is largely spongy bone in order to act as a shock absorber (Fig. 176). Fractures, then, are usually crushing in nature.

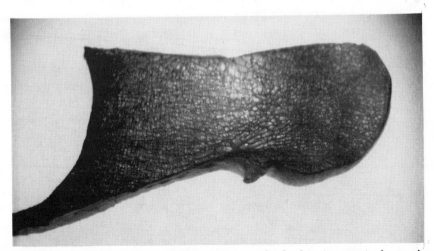

Fig. 176. A transilluminated thin section of the body of a cervical vertebra to show the complex (and beautiful) interlacing of the bony trabeculae.

WOBBLER

The clinical signs of wobbler are difficult to describe and even more difficult to differentiate from certain other conditions that affect the spinal cord of the horse. (For details, see the references given in the Preface.) Briefly, the young horse shows signs of ataxia (incoordination) primarily involving the rearlegs. He sways loosely from side to side and seems incapable of controlling the action and placing of the rearlegs. As seen from the rear the gait is best described as a "drunken stagger." Mild degrees of incoordination of this sort may be very difficult to detect and appear to the horseman as "funny going behind." An accurate diagnosis can only be made by the experienced veterinarian, and he may have to examine the animal several times over a period of several weeks before the diagnosis can be arrived at with certainty.

In brief, there is a malformation of one or more neck vertebrae which allows those vertebrae to move too much (subluxate), one on the other, during flexion of the neck. The subluxation results in pressure on the spinal cord in the neck which causes destruction of the white matter of the spinal cord, and, consequently, clinical signs of ataxia or incoordination. Although I cannot consider this in detail, I do think you ought to have some idea how the vertebrae become malformed. The neck of the horse is made up of a series of seven vertebrae. The head hangs on the end of this column or beam. Mechanically, this is what is called a cantilever beam. To really follow my argument, obtain seven small blocks of wood and glue them together with a piece of soft rubber between each piece. Attach a small weight to one end and hold the other end. You will see that the column tends to deflect, move more toward the free end. If you now fix two pieces of cardboard, as shown (Fig. 177), and allow the deflection to occur, you will see that the cardboards are pressed together. The cardboards represent the intervertebral joints. If pressed together like this for a time, damage will be done to the developing little joints. This damage leads to overgrowth of the joint (Figs. 178, 179) through an osteochondrosis process, as I have discussed previously. When the joint is overgrown, is bigger than it should be, the vertebrae can move on each other more than normal, resulting in subluxation and pressure on the spinal cord. If you make the column longer, the deflection will be more and more obvious, with more of a tendency for abnormal pressure, more chance of spinal cord damage and wobbles. The longer the neck and the heavier the head, the greater chance there is for wobbles to develop. As noted earlier, man has been selecting for this.

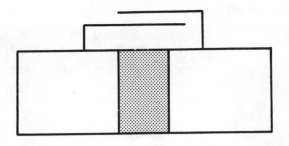

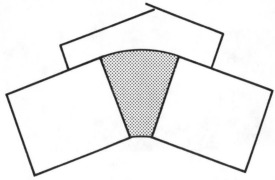

Fig. 177. A simple model to show the working of the intervertebral joints. See the text for explanation.

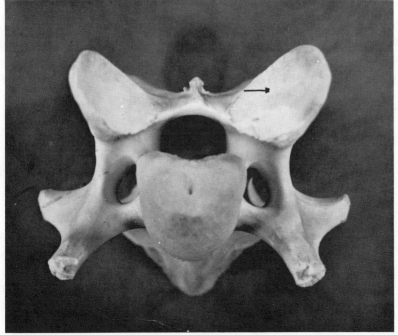

Fig. 178. Head on view of a wobbler vertebra. The articular process marked with the arrow is larger than normal.

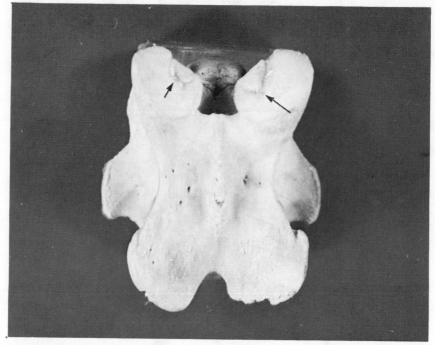

Fig. 179. Top view of a wobbler vertebra. Both articular processes are enlarged and show osteochondrosis (arrows).

Once a wobbler, always a wobbler. The spinal cord damage is permanent. An animal with such damage, however, can learn to compensate to some extent if the damage is not too severe. Some people claim to cure wobbles with diets, controlled exercise, etc. The animal can learn to compensate to some degree. The sad fact is, however, that these are dangerous animals to ride. As they tire, the compensation is lost, the wobbles reappear, and the animal is apt to misstep or fall, hurting himself and/or the rider.

I mentioned that long necks are also associated with roaring, that form of broken wind caused by paralysis of the muscles on the left side of the larynx. Again, the details are beyond our scope but can be found in the references. Put simply, the left recurrent nerve supplies the motor nerves to the left side of the larynx while the right recurrent supplies the right. The left nerve is longer because it wraps around the aorta, the main artery leaving the heart. Mechanically it can be shown that the longer the neck the greater tension is exerted on the nerves, and there is always greater tension on the left nerve. Tension, as I have talked about earlier, can damage nerves. The long neck, therefore, puts more tension on the left recurrent nerve, leading to nerve damage, muscle paralysis, and roaring. (Giraffes do not have recurrent nerves of this type, and therefore, do not roar!)

There are a number of other conditions that affect the horse's brain and spinal cord: encephalitis, myelitis, etc. Since there is nothing you can do about these conditions, I do not think I will go into them here. You can read more about them in the references given in the Preface.

SPONDYLOSIS DEFORMANS OR COLD BACK

This is not uncommon in horses. It occurs, as a rule, near the middle of the vertebral column, thoracic vertebrae 12, 13, and it occurs because of downward bending of the vertebral column, as I talked about earlier (Fig. 180). This downward bending results in tearing of the outer, lower part of the intervertebral disk with subsequent new bone formation on the bottom of the vertebrae (Fig. 181). These new bone formations eventually bridge across the vertebrae, splinting them, so that further bending does not occur. At the same time the intervertebral joints are jammed together and may, eventually, fuse (Fig. 182).

We see this sort of bone bridging rather often in older horses, particularly if they have been hunters or jumpers. It may be assumed that at the time the tearing occurred, and the new bone was forming, there was pain, so-called *cold back*. Once the new bone bridges have formed and/or the small joints are fused (leading to the same thing: a rigid, no longer moving back segment) the pain disappears.

The dorsal spines will tend to move together as a result of this bending. Noting this, some surgeons blame it all (cold back, that is) on the spines pressing together, and therefore, remove them surgically. Good results are said to follow, but this is difficult to assess since most cold backs repair themselves in time, the pain disappearing as soon as the fusion and bridging is completed. I should be inclined to wait.

The clinical signs of cold back can be quite difficult to assess. In general, the animal does not perform well, may refuse jumps, and resents (more than usual) the saddle girth. Often people will squeeze or pinch along either side of the spines of the backbone; the horse dorsiflexes his back (bends the back down). This is a normal reflex (vertebra prominens) in the horse and can be variably obvious from animal to animal. Also, finger pressure on either side of the withers may be strongly resented by many horses and says nothing about cold back. It is a difficult diagnosis to make; one should get the best help one can.

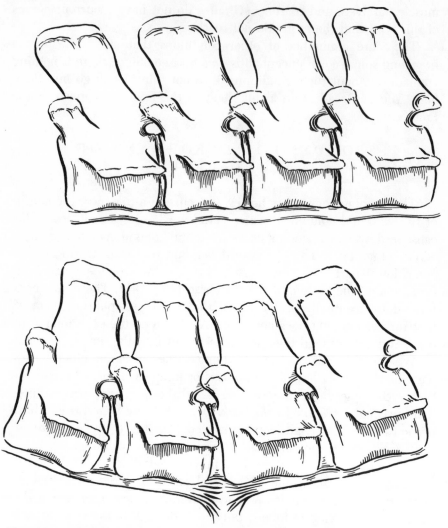

Fig. 180. This shows the downward bending of the vertebrae (dorsiflexion) which tears the ventral ligaments, resulting in spondylosis deformans. Above is normal position and below is dorsiflexion and tearing.

INFECTION OF JOINTS

Although infection of joints, bursae, etc. do occasionally occur in working age animals, they are most important in the foal. Since infections of this nature can effectively destroy an animal's working usefulness, it is reasonable that I consider them in this book.

The major known causes of joint infection in foals are the bacteria:

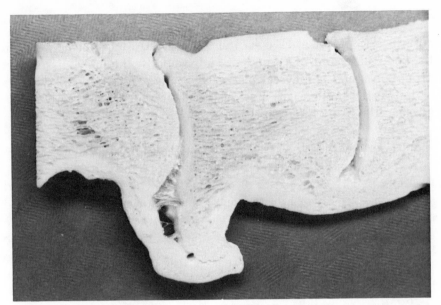

Fig. 181. Three vertebrae that have been fused together on their ventral surfaces (lower surfaces). The spur on the left is very obvious, but the two vertebrae on the right are fused as well.

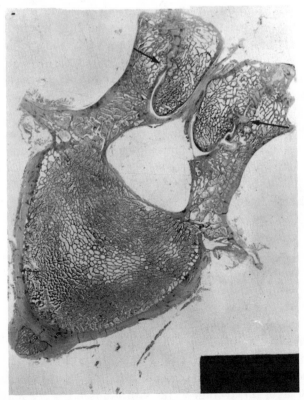

Fig. 182. A cross section showing two intervertebral joints fused together (arrows). The joint spaces remaining are just beneath the arrows.

Shigella, Streptococci, E. coli, and Salmonella. Any joint or joints in the body may be involved and, not infrequently, the infection may set up in bones and epiphyseal plates. The larger joints and those joints closest to the midline are most often involved: shoulder, hock, stifle, hip, and the many little joints in the vertebral column.

All of these organisms gain entrance to the body by two major routes: the mouth and intestinal tract or the umbilicus. A rare case is introduced through the respiratory system, nose and lungs. Prevention, therefore, is largely a matter of exacting, rigid sanitation. In the wild state horses are always on the move, not living in sharply delimited areas where these organisms can accumulate and so saturate the environment that foals routinely become infected. Since we limit the horse's range, we must do the best we can to see that the range (paddocks, barns, whatever) is as clean as possible. Once into the body, the organisms travel through the bloodstream to reach the joints.

Painting the umbilicus with some form of disinfectant is a common practice in order to prevent entrance of bacteria into the umbilical area. I believe it is useless. The iodine may kill the organisms present at the time you paint it on, but it does not prevent a whole new crop accumulating an hour later. In fact, if you use strong tincture of iodine, you can seal off the umbilicus, sealing in the organisms, so that they form an abscess inside the body (in the urachus). The umbilicus is supposed to weep for a few days. Nature constructed it to weep, and the weeping fluid keeps washing bacteria away as and if they accumulate. It is exactly the same sort of thing as the constant movement of mucus up the respiratory system to protect the lungs from infection. If the weeping persists more than a few days, have a veterinarian examine the animal. It may have a patent urachus (a persistence of the connection of the urinary bladder to the umbilicus).

Shigella (or E. coli: they act very much the same) causes an acute febrile disease in the young foal, primarily during the first two weeks of life. They become very sick, and will die unless treated quickly and thoroughly. Any sick foal during the first two weeks should be considered to have a Shigella infection until proved otherwise. Often the horseman sees a foal with a swollen joint or limb and believes that he was kicked by a mare. Usually this is not the case, and it is always best to think in terms of infection. Call your veterinarian; Shigella is nothing to play around with. Even if the joints are infected by Shigella, they will return completely to normal if the animal is treated properly (Fig. 183).

Streptococci can infect the foal anytime from birth to about two months of age, on average. The symptoms are very similar to those

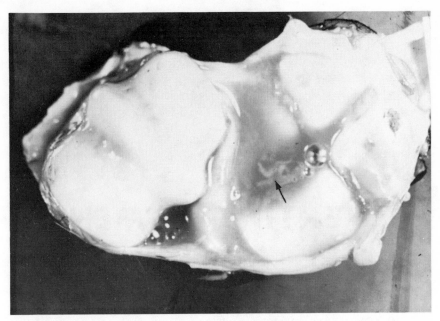

Fig. 183. A fetlock joint from a foal with joint-ill. The synovial fluid should be clear but is turbid and full of pus (arrow) as a result of bacterial infection.

of Shigella but may be somewhat less acute and violent. This bacterium does cause extensive and severe destruction of the joint cartilage, and the animal may be useless even if he survives. Many horsemen try to treat such foals themselves and thereby compound the problem. Antibiotics must be administered properly and for a long period to insure that the infection is completely cleared up. A few days of penicillin may clear the strep from the bloodstream, but it will lodge in the joints, where the antibiotic cannot reach it as well, and cause a recurrence of the joint infection a week to ten days later. As a rule of thumb, antibiotics should be given for a minimum of five to seven days.

Salmonella infections usually start in somewhat older animals, one to three months of age, in general. Such infections typically present as a severe diarrhea involving a number of foals, unlike the single case occurrence of both Shigella and Streptococci. A few days to a week or so after the bout of diarrhea, joint infections appear in a few of the affected animals. It is fortunate that only a few foals of the affected group develop joint infections because they are terrible to deal with, destroy joint cartilage in the same fashion as the Streptococcus, and usually end up destroying the joint completely. Again, immediate veterinary attention should be sought whenever diarrhea occurs in young foals.

6
PREVENTING LAMENESS

IN THIS CONCLUDING CHAPTER I SHOULD LIKE TO SUM UP AND CODIFY some of the ideas presented about the prevention of lameness. Treatment, in most cases, consists of skillful neglect; what we must do is prevent.

One of the most intelligent things I have ever heard about preventing lameness came from a racehorse trainer—John Jacobs. The policy in his breeding-racing operation, and that of his famous father before him, is to race and sell fast, lame horses; race and keep fast, sound horses. A simple and brilliant genetic rule: do not select for speed alone, looks alone, ears or tails alone; select for what you want plus soundness. All my talk about conformation boils down to this. Even if you do not know anything about conformation, you can recognize a lame horse!

Quarter Horse people, I have been hard on you, and, I think, with justification. On the other hand, your animals are, generally, nice folks to deal with. Now, if you will just do something about the conformation! A good, strong body is fine, but there must be legs and feet to match.

Arabian, Appaloosa, Palomino people; do not go on looks alone! You end up with cerebellar hypoplasia, weird skin tumors, congenital muscle diseases. The horse must perform as a locomotor animal. Performance is the yardstick for strong individuals and strong breeds.

I shall never be able to accept with any equanimity the artificial standards so frequently applied to the performance of the horse. He is, basically, a moderate-speed, long-distance runner, not a flashy, five gaiter or a highrise jumper. I know very well that you are going

228

to jump him. That is fair enough. If you cannot do what you want, why have him? But, accept the fact that what you ask the horse to do may hurt him. Select for strong individuals and train them carefully and well.

Show horses and Tennessee Walking Horses are something else, not to mention Hackney ponies. Why in heaven's name set standards of performance, standards of excellence that require horrendous feet, thick pads, warhorse shoes, and mutilated tails? Natural is beautiful, too!

One thing hunter and show people accomplish, of necessity, that the racehorse fraternity should learn. They do train their horses for manners, leads, and how to get along reasonably well with man. There are many racehorse trainers who really do not know which lead a horse should take going around a turn. It is a joy to visit Newmarket, England, for example, and see the strings of Thoroughbreds walking calmly through the streets of the town on their way to the morning exercise. They have manners. Compare the American Thoroughbreds who have to be led to the track and pointed in the right direction by lead ponies.

Let's talk now about tracks and surfaces. Everybody blames track surfaces for their troubles and, in many cases, rightly so. What is the ideal surface on which to race or work a horse? It is, obviously, the surface he was on in the wild: plains country with a soil laced with grass roots holding moisture—in other words an elastic, somewhat spongy surface that yields to the hoof and springs back again.

My thoughts on this subject were singularly stimulated by a walk one day over the heaths and gallops of Newmarket. There is a gallop there called the invalid gallop. You cannot see it, but you can feel it. Peat moss has been spread on this gallop for many, many years, and the soil is springy, elastic, lovely to walk on. Wouldn't all horses like to work on such a surface!

How does one accomplish this? For the training track, show ring: peat moss, peat moss, and more peat moss. The racetrack presents different problems. Under American racing conditions, at least, the track must be maintained for weeks and even months at a time for daily racing. What does one do about that?

Several years ago I made a suggestion, the response to which was completely underwhelming. The idea shown in Fig. 184 was developed. Dig out the track and throw away all the magic sand and clay. Fill the trench with a mixture of soil and peat moss or some synthetic substitute for peat moss. Provide a moisture measurement system, so that the track can be watered, or allowed to drain, to near constant moisture content. One of the advantages of the peat, or grass

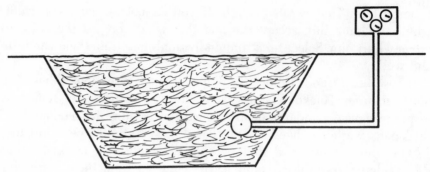

Fig. 184. Cross section of proposed working, racing surface for horses. See the text for details.

roots, is to hold moisture levels near constant, and the moisture content has a great deal to do with the elasticity. The precise proportions of peat and soil, the type of soil, proportion of moisture, would all have to be worked out experimentally, and could be worked out.

Maintenance problems should be no greater than with the conventional track surface. If nothing else, the corduroy ridges and grooves of the tractors and harrows would be eliminated. At the same time the divot danger of the turf course could be avoided by light harrowing. Perhaps the surface formulation could even be so set that the hoof could cut in without divoting.

Concerning the present plastic tracks I can only cringe. The hoof cannot cut in and that is just not right! There is, also, a tremendous build-up of heat immediately above the plastic surface, and, surely, the hoof does not need that.

Ideally, we should not race around turns, but we must. Most turns on racetracks seemed to have been designed by guess and neglect. There is abundant engineering technology available on how to bank turns for wheeled vehicles, two or four. I am sure a good highway engineer could apply this knowledge readily to horse tracks. I might suggest to them that since horse's joints move on three dimensional log spiral pathways, the turns might be constructed in the same way (Fig. 185). The log spiral radius decreases on the way into the turn and increases on the way out of the turn. In cross section (Fig. 186) the radius decreases toward the top of the turn.

Horseshoes and horseshoeing: I have already said a great deal on the subject. Let me quote from a great and intelligent harness horse trainer, Frank Ervin, "I have seen about everything there is with respect to freak shoes and trick balancing techniques. I have tried a great many of these things myself but in the long run, *short*

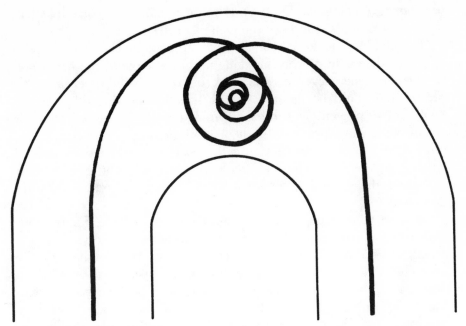

Fig. 185. Suggested log spiral pathway for racetrack turns, aerial view. The highly curved parts would not be present, of course, and the two curves would be smoothed and blended at the top of the figure.

Fig. 186. Suggested log spiral pathway for racetrack turns, cross section view. The inside rail is to the left and the outside fence to the right. The highly curved part would not be present, of course, and is included (as in Fig. 185) only to indicate that the surface is a log spiral.

toe and light weight are the keys. If you can achieve balance by sticking to that formula, you have the game half-licked."

I should like to add only one further suggestion. The main purpose of a horseshoe is to prevent breaking up of the edge of the hoof wall. Could not some clever person work on the possibility of a tough plastic that could be painted on the trimmed bearing edge of the hoof wall to prevent such breaking up? It could be rasped away or cut off with fine nippers as the hoof grows and then replaced. Trimming would be necessary because the coating would reduce normal wearing of the hoof. The hoof could then cut into the ground as it should, if the ground is made in some manner natural, as already described.

It is certainly true, as innumerable authorities have pointed out, that we know less about the nutritional needs of the horse than any other domestic species. I do not accept, however, the corollary usually presented that we do not know how to feed horses. Just because we do not know why we are doing something does not necessarily mean that we are doing it wrong. Both man and the horse managed somehow to evolve from the primeval slime without any particular intellectual understanding of what they were doing. I hasten to say that I am not opposed to intensive, careful research on nutrition in horses. When the work is done, however, I venture to predict that grass, hay (yes, even timothy), and oats will stand untarnished in the scientific array.

On the basis of my experience the worst nutritional disease of the horse is too much nutrition. Overfeeding with high caloric rations does more harm than any other single nutritional factor. That fact has been detailed in many places throughout this volume.

Apart from overfeeding there are only three precisely defined nutritional diseases of the horse of which I am aware. The first, nutritional hyperparathyroidism, has been discussed. There must be a balance between the amounts of calcium and phosphorus which a horse eats. Under natural pasture conditions the animal can usually take care of the problem for himself. With certain soils in certain parts of the world and with hand feeding, man must pay attention to this factor. The second nutritional condition is purely man-made. Horses, or anything else for that matter, can have too high an intake of vitamin D. Excessive vitamin D will cause widespread calcification of blood vessels, tendons, and ligaments, rendering the horse useless or dead. If one is going to provide a vitamin supplement, supply only one, not five or ten. A little bit is good and a lot can do a lot of harm. This is particularly true of the fat soluble vitamins, A and D.

The third condition is vitamin E—selenium deficiency which, rarely in the United States, at least, causes damage to skeletal muscles.

Finally we come to the subject of too early working of young horses. I do not subscribe to the oversimplification that *all* working of *all* young horses is bad. There is no question that in both human and horse the immature are often better athletes than the mature. Better athletes, that is, in one sense—let me try to make that clear. There are basically two requirements for athletic performance: innate ability and learned ability. Innate ability such as speed may be best expressed in the younger individual. Learned ability such as showing at prescribed gaits, jumping over obstacles, is best expressed in the older individual. That is clear enough: we flat race the young horse and jump the older horse.

Given a well-built young horse with good conformation, nothing such as upright pasterns or sickle hocks to predispose him to damage, most lamenesses will be a function of what man asks the horse to do. If he asks him to run full out for three furlongs in a field of eighteen other terrified youngsters, he may hurt himself. If before putting him in that cavalry charge, however, the young horse is taught (the learned ability) to change leads, taught to pull up or go on signal, taught, in short, how to race, there is less chance that he will be hurt. Do we really train the young Thoroughbred to race? I think not. We put him on the track, point him in the right direction and go like blazes.

The early training and racing (and that is what I am talking about, primarily) of the young horse, then, is not necessarily bad. What is bad is that we do not properly prepare the horse for that racing.

Finally: select for good conformation, feed adequately but do not overdo, let the foot be as natural as possible, train carefully, work wisely—and good luck!

INDEX